CLASSICBEER

LAMBIC

THE BEER SHOP
14, PITFIELD ST
LONDON N1 6EY
TEL: 0171 7393701

JEAN-XAVIER GUINARD

 A Brewers Publications Book

Lambic
By Jean-Xavier Guinard
Classic Beer Style Series
Edited by Virginia Thomas
Copyright 1990 by Jean-Xavier Guinard

ISBN: 0-937381-22-5
Printed in the United States of America
10 9 8 7 6 5

Published by Brewers Publications,
a division of the Association of Brewers.
PO Box 1679, Boulder, Colorado 80306-1679 USA
(303) 447-0816 • FAX: (303) 447-2825

Direct all inquiries/orders to the above address.

Cover design by Robert L. Schram
Cover photography by Michael Lichter, Michael Lichter Photography
Cask courtesy of North Denver Cellar

To Cristina

TABLE OF CONTENTS

Acknowledgements

My deepest appreciation is extended to Professor Michael Lewis, my brewing teacher, for supporting this enterprise.

I am grateful to Jean-Pierre and Claude Van Roy (Brasserie Cantillon and Musée Bruxellois de la Gueuze) who provided a wealth of information for this text.

I am pleased to acknowledge the assistance and contributions of the following researchers, students and brewers: Professor H. Verachtert (Katholieke Universiteit, Leuven), Professor Herman Phaff (University of California, Davis), Eric Hamacher and Malcolm McDonald (University of California, Davis), René Lindemans (Brasserie Lindemans), Henny Fonteyn (Brasserie Belle-Vue), Robert Everaerts and M. Van Campenhout (Brouwerij De Neve), Christian Berger (La Microbrasserie, Paris), and Jan De Brabanter (Confédération des Brasseries de Belgique).

Were it not for Thierry Claudon, I might never have developed a passion for lambic beers. My thanks to Charlie Papazian for giving me the opportunity to write about them.

About the Author

Born on the 4th of July, 1961, and bred in Paris, France, Jean-Xavier Guinard has lived in the United States and enjoyed the fireworks for his birthday for the last 7 years. He holds a degree in Food and Agricultural Engineering from the French Institute of Brewing in Nancy, a master's degree in Sensory Science from the University of Paris, and a master's degree in Enology from UC Davis. He is currently finishing his Ph.D. in Microbiology under Michael Lewis at UC Davis.

Jean-Xavier Guinard teaches undergraduate and extension courses in Food Science in the U.S. and in France and has worked in the wine and beer industries in Europe. A member of the Master Brewers Association of the Americas and of the American Society for Enology and Viticulture, he is the author of several scientific publications in sensory science, brewing, enology and microbiology.

Jean-Xavier plans to open a California-style brewpub in Paris soon. To him, Belgium is paradise for beers. He loves soccer, classical music, Sierra Nevada's Pale Ale . . . and lambics.

Introduction

Once a student of biology in Paris, I remember being dragged away from my books one night by a good friend. He took me to the Pinte, a typical pub of the Quartier Latin, with dozens of beers on tap and live entertainment. This friend of mine, Epicurean and down to earth in nature, knew a great deal about beer, a strength I valued much less at the time than those of being well-read, fluent in Latin, at ease with mathematics, and generally well-regarded by members of the opposite sex. When we sat down at the bar, I let him order for us as usual. The week having brought poor grades and dreadful assignments, he suggested I try a kriek.

"A what ?" I asked.

"A kriek," he repeated. "It's a wheat beer from Belgium made by spontaneous fermentation and with macerated cherries."

Upon looking up at the board listing the prices of the beers on tap, I glanced at him and asked if he was kidding.

"No. I am not!" he said. "It's worth it; it's the best beer in the world, and I am buying!"

I watched the bartender place the rim of the tilted glass (which was huge) against the tap, and a burgundy red, bubbly liquid flowed down into it, producing a white foam tinged with pink, which the bartender made sure not to waste. There I sat in front of my glass of kriek, my friend eagerly waiting for his.

What followed was a unique sensory experience. The beer had a notably smooth and full body and a creaminess that my friend related to the stable foam and medium carbonation. It was quite sour and acetic, a trifle on the sweet side, with hints of cheesy aroma against a woody background and lots of cherry aroma that seemed to fill the room. The finish was dry and cidery. Needless to say, I did not pick up all these unusual attributes myself. My friend pointed them out to me one by one. Something I could smell, however, but not describe, was later identified by him as the characteristic aroma of the yeast *Brettanomyces*, which I had never heard of before, convinced as I was that only *Saccharomyces* could change wort into beer. Yet, he told me, *Brettanomyces* is unique to the fermentation process of lambics, the family of beers to which kriek belongs.

Lambic is the only beer of its kind in the world. It is made by spontaneous fermentation of a wort produced from 40 percent unmalted wheat and 60 percent barley malt. Mashing follows a temperature profile. The temperature is increased by one or two decoctions of portions of the mash and by additions of boiling water. The wort is boiled for at least three hours with aged (*surannés*) hops that have lost their bittering power but have retained their antiseptic properties. Lambic is brewed mostly within ten miles of the city of Brussels, because the proper microbial flora is found only in that limited area. Production is concentrated in the western districts of Brussels, spreading out into the nearby farming villages collectively known as Payottenland. Traditionally, lambic is brewed only from October 15 to May 15 because high summer temperatures can spoil the

Man with Glass of Beer. David Teniers. Musée du Louvre, Paris, France.

fermentations. The inoculation of the wort with the local microbial flora is achieved by letting the hot wort cool overnight in a wide and shallow cooling tun (*bac refroidissoir*) which leaves a large wort surface area in contact with the atmosphere. The next morning, the wort is pumped into wooden casks (*tonnes, pipes,* and *foudres* ranging in capacity from two to twenty-five barrels), in which it picks up some additional microorganisms among those lodged in the wood from previous uses.

The fermentation involves a sequence of yeasts and

bacteria, the combined action of which produces over a period of several months a lambic that is fruity, acetic, and sour but not bitter. It starts three to seven days after the wort has been cooled, with the development of *Kloeckera* yeasts and enteric bacteria that produce large amounts of acetic acid. After two to three weeks, these organisms are overgrown by *Saccharomyces cerevisiae* yeasts that complete the main alcoholic fermentation in three to four months. A strong bacterial activity is observed next with strains of the lactic acid bacteria *Pediococcus* and *Lactobacillus*. As their names indicate, these bacteria produce tremendous amounts of lactic acid and cause a large pH drop in the wort. After five to eight months, a new population of yeasts of the species *Brettanomyces bruxellensis* and *Brettanomyces lambicus* appears in the fermenting lambic wort. These yeasts further reduce the residual extract and give the lambic its unique flavor. Lambics of different ages are then blended and bottled to make *gueuze*.

A secondary fermentation takes place in the bottle, as in the *méthode Champenoise* used to make Champagne. For this fermentation to occur and to produce the right flavor and amount of carbon dioxide, the brewer must skillfully blend his lambics to achieve the right amount of fermentable extract in the bottle. It takes at least a year in the bottle to make a good gueuze (6 to 8 percent alcohol by volume). Some breweries and cafés offer sweetened young *(fox)* lambic called *lambic doux* fresh out of the cask. A few breweries also produce a version of lambic that has been aged for three years in wood and one year in the bottle. This version, called *vieux lambic* (old lambic), is devoid of carbon dioxide and is sour and very dry.

In the old days, the lambic brewer used to make *faro* by blending lambics produced from high- and low-gravity worts, respectively. Faro was served with a lump of sugar in the glass (like absinthe). Today, faro is a lambic made from moderate-gravity wort (6 to 8 degrees Plato), sweetened with candy sugar. The lambic produced from the late, low-gravity worts was called *mars* beer. People from Brussels drank it at home with their family, but rarely at the pub, and today *mars* beer is no longer commercialized.

Fruit derivatives of lambic (*kriek, framboise, cassis, pêche,* and *muscat* or *"druiven"*) surely have their origins in the days before hops were used in beer. They are produced by macerating whole fruits with a blend of young lambics (about fifty pounds of fruit per barrel of lambic) into wooden casks and bottling the resulting beer after six months with a dose of young lambic to allow for an additional fermentation in the bottle.

1

History of Lambic Beers

THE BELGIAN BREWING TRADITION

The very old brewing tradition of Belgium offers the most numerous, diverse, and individualistic brews in the world. To quote the bard Emile Verhaeren, "In Belgium, the magistrate has the dignity of a prince but by Bacchus, it is true that the brewer is king."

Brewing technology was introduced in Belgium by the Celts. In those days, beer was generally brewed by women. Beer was considered a food and also was consumed because surface water frequently was polluted. In the sixth century, monks began to take a very keen interest in brewing and in developing new brewing practices, for example, by adding herbs and spices to the wort. The brewing skill in Belgium was to remain the exclusive privilege of abbeys until the twelfth century. Arnold, a Benedictine monk and distinguished brewer, founded St. Peter's Abbey at Oudenburg, near Ostende, in the late 1000s. He was canonized after his death and became the patron saint of Belgian brewers.

Towards the end of the Middle Ages, brewing gradually became a middle-class craft and gave rise to powerful, influential guilds. The first guild of brewers dates back to 1303. In 1357, the first trade association was founded in the city of Liège, and applicants were carefully scrutinized before being granted membership. Illegitimate children, people convicted of concubinage and those who had been excommunicated were excluded. Brewing apprentices were required to produce a certificate of good conduct and to pay registration dues before being admitted. For the first time, strict rules were laid down for the commerce of beer. In Brussels, brewers who used illegal adjuncts and prohibited practices risked being burned at the stake.

In the seventeenth and eighteenth centuries, the brewer was considered an artisan in largely agrarian communities. Local farmers supplied grain to the brewery in exchange for kegs of beer on a simple credit system. The spent grains were returned to the farmers for winter feed, and the brewer sold his surplus to local taverns for profit. The brewer kept track of the transactions in a ledger. A look at these accounts shows that the farmers consumed a lot of beer and often were in the brewer's debt. Alternatively, some breweries were also farms. The workforce was used in the fields in the spring and summer months to care for and harvest the crops, and in the brewery the rest of the year to malt the barley and brew the beer. This is another reason why lambic is traditionally brewed only between October and May. It also explains why lambic was once written off as a "farmers' drink."

LAMBIC, AN ANCESTRAL BREWING METHOD

Lambic brewing is the oldest brewing method still in use in the Western world. As pointed out by Marcel Gocar, a Belgian brewing expert and historian, there are striking similarities between *sikaru*, the beer produced 5,000 years ago in Mesopotamia by Sumerians, and lambic. An ancient Sumerian tablet in cuneiform writing reveals that the basic composition of sikaru was virtually identical to that of today's lambic. Indeed, Sumerian brewer Amarkiskar used sixty "silas" of barley malt and thirty six "silas" of a Sumerian variety of wheat called *épeautre*, that is, 62.5 percent malt and 37.5 percent raw grain. Today, to brew his lambic at Cantillon, Jean-Pierre Van Roy uses 1,830 pounds (830 kg) of barley malt and 1,014 pounds (460 kg) of unmalted wheat, which comes to 65 percent malt and 35 percent raw grain. Lambic wort is boiled with aged hops, which contribute some aroma but no bitterness. The hop was not known to Sumerians and Amarkiskar used spices such as cinnamon to add flavor to his sikaru.

The spontaneous fermentation of the sikaru wort was triggered by the local microbial flora of wild *Saccharomyces* and *Schizosaccharomyces* yeasts. *Schizosaccharomyces* is the only yeast that reproduces by fission instead of budding. It ferments glucose and maltose very well, and to a lesser extent some dextrins, and it is resistant to high levels of acetic acid, a property of importance at times when beers were almost always infected with acetic acid-producing yeasts and bacteria. Similarly, the spontaneous fermentation of lambic wort involves the local microbial flora of enteric and lactic acid bacteria and *Saccharomyces* and *Brettanomyces* yeasts, which altogether produce high amounts of acetic and lactic acids.

Finally, both sikaru and lambic or its derivatives are luxury items. The Sumerian tablet mentions that the sikaru formulation yielded premium quality beer. Sikaru was used as payment of the salaries and fees of both the working class and their managers. Gueuze is often called the "Burgundy of beers" or "Brussels Champagne," and kriek or framboise are regarded as very refined and sophisticated beverages. These beers are rather expensive except when they are purchased locally. A pint of draft lambic at a pub in one of the small towns around Brussels is about fifty cents. However, a bottle of gueuze, kriek or framboise runs about six dollars in Paris, the city with the greatest selection of lambic beers in the world after Brussels. Similar prices apply in the United States where the selection is very limited.

ETYMOLOGY OF TERMS

According to a writer from the *Tirailleur* newspaper in 1883, the term *lambic* has its origin in the peasants' belief that lambic, being very harsh to the palate, was a distilled beverage. The peasants would often call it the *alambic*, in reference to the distilling apparatus. Belgian historian Godefroi Kurth agrees that lambic derives from alambic, but according to him, alambic was the old name for the mashing vessel used to brew lambic beer. The dictionary of the Academy of Gastronomy suggests that the etymology of the term *lambic* is found in the Latin verb *lambere* meaning to sip. It could also be that lambic, which often appears as lambiek, is derived from the village of Lembeek in Payottenland.

As for the term *faro*, it comes from the Spanish words *farro* meaning barley wine, a wine from Portugal, or a lighthouse. Indeed, Belgian rumor has it that after drinking a few pints of faro, people would become very enlightening. Faro was the main drink in Belgium in the nineteenth century. In 1855, a two-cent increase in the price of a glass of faro almost caused a riot among "Brusseleers" for whom the daily mug of faro was a necessity. A group of actors from famous cabarets even staged a play to denounce the price hike.

The gueuze appellation was born in Lembecq, a small town outside Brussels, which was very fortunate not to have to pay any excise tax on the brews it produced until 1860. In 1870, the mayor of Lembecq, who owned a brewery, hired an engineer by the name of Cayaerts. Together, they decided to apply the *méthode Champenoise* to referment lambic beer in a bottle. Gueuze was born. This new invention was called "lambic from the gueux" because the liberal ideas of the mayor were those of the political party of the gueux. The lambic of the gueux soon became known as *gueuze*. According to Dutch writer Anton Van Duinkerken, the term gueuze more simply originated during the War of the Gueux in the sixteenth century.

Finally, *kriek* is Flemish for cherry, and *framboise* is French for raspberry.

LAMBIC, PART OF THE BELGIAN WAY OF LIFE

The importance of lambic beers in Belgium's everyday life is emphasized in Belgian art, literature and gastronomy. The simplicity and refinement of lambic beers is in the tradition of the works by the great Flemish masters. Their paintings, which mixed realism and poetry, radiate a peculiar mixture of proud self-confidence and jovial love of life in their representation of the festive atmosphere of seventeenth century taverns. The depiction of beery excess by Brueghel The Elder and, after him, Teniers the Younger and Jacob Joardens demonstrates the familiarity of these painters with Belgian brews. A strong conviviality is apparent in the *Village Fair* scenes by Pierre Paul Rubens and Peter Brueghel the Younger. The aptly named Brauwer, an elegant gentleman of intellectual culture who turned buffoon and died at the age of thirty-two, painted many coarse scenes in low taverns where lambic flowed freely. The *Flemish Party* is another illustration of festive beer drinking by the son of a brewer, Jan Steen, himself brewer and tavern owner at one time. His

Village Wedding. By Pieter Brueghel, The Elder. Museum, Vienna, Austria.

art studies led him from tavern to tavern, and many of his paintings represent voluptuous waitresses serving ever-thirsty customers. There is little doubt that if we could reach for one of the stoneware pots of beer painted by these masters and taste its contents, we would recognize the acidic and fruity flavor of lambic.

Lambic beers have inspired many writers, although not always in the best of ways. It is not known whether his love for wine or the complete failure of the series of conferences he gave in Belgium made the French poet Baudelaire so resentful of lambic beers. Even though lambic is not everyone's drink, one can only be surprised by the definitive and expeditious judgement of faro by the author of the *Fleurs du Mal*, who wrote, "Faro is drawn from the great latrine, the Senne; it is a beverage extracted from the excrements of the city through its sewer system. That is how the city has been drinking its own urine for centuries."

Belgian poets and writers have understandably been

much kinder to lambic beers. The great Walloon poet Emile Verhaeren wrote many verses on their virtues. In 1863, faro was definitely the main character in Ch. Flor O'Squarr's play *Ouye. Ouye.. Ouye...* staged at the Galeries St-Hubert Theater in Brussels. From the play, we learn that a glass of faro cost fifteen *centimes* (cents) at the time (most likely in a very fancy café). The *Memoirs of Jef Lambic,* however, are the most notorious piece of "lambic" literature. The story has it that the memoirs were discovered during the demolition of an old Brussels mansion to make room for the building of a swimming pool. Workers collapsed the wall of a hidden cellar and found a small wooden cask that they trusted to city officials. Much to their disappointment, the cask did not contain any liquid treasure, but instead a manuscript carefully wrapped in women's pink and blue garters. The label on the manuscript read *"Memoirs of a Pottezuyper,* by Jef Lambic."* The memoirs give an interesting account of life in Brussels in the late 1800s and show how it was customary for people to meet after work in cafés over the traditional glasses of lambic and faro. They also describe the scare among lambic brewers caused in the 1860s by the emergence of German bottom-fermented lagers on the Belgian market. Jef Lambic was an avid drinker of lambic beers and a good man. Suffice it to say that he lived ninety-one years and that all 1,756 empty gueuze bottles and forty-nine empty lambic or faro casks recovered from his cellar were auctioned at his death to benefit the city's orphanage.

In Belgium, beer was used as a flavoring agent in family home cooking for centuries. This tradition was replaced in 1830 with the French practice of cooking with wine. Cooking with beer did not come back into style until 1955. The Belgian rationale for cooking with beer is not to impart to the dish a beery taste, but rather to enhance the original flavor of the dish through the moderate use of beer.

Notorious Belgian dishes prepared with gueuze or lambic include Albert Vossen's eels, Curnonsky's Choesels (beef or veal pancreas) and Flemish Carbonnades (beef stew), Raoul Morleghem's Pork Meat Pie, Uylenspiegel Fowl, and Brewmasters' Witloof. Morleghem also offers delicious recipes with kriek such as Cherry Duckling and Saint-Michel Cherry Pie. Gueuze also is regarded as an excellent tonic and was prescribed many times by doctors during war times. The best tonic of all is a simple cocktail made with egg yolk, sugar, and gueuze.

THE LAMBIC BREWING INDUSTRY

As in most countries, the production of beer in Belgium is now concentrated around a few large brewing groups. This concentration movement has not stopped new, small, artisanal breweries from arising, however. The explanation for that phenomenon lies in the resurgence of specialty beer drinkers. This definite trend also has incited medium-sized lager breweries to begin producing specialty beers, while the big brewing groups have gotten themselves a large part of the specialty beers market by takeovers of existing breweries. The two major Belgian breweries (Stella Artois and Maes Pils) and other large European breweries (Whitbread) are slowly but surely swallowing up local competitors. The number of small, family-operated breweries has shrunk from more than 3,000 in 1900 to as few as 60 today.

According to the Belgian Brewers' Association, the lambic brewing industry has not escaped major concentrations. At the beginning of this century, there still were some fifty lambic brewers in the Brussels area and about eighty in the Senne Valley. Today, about twenty lambic breweries remain, plus a number of small firms (blenders) that buy their wort from bigger breweries and then attend to the

LES MEMOIRES
DE
JEF LAMBIC

DESSINS
DE
Robert DESART

PREFACE
DE
Léon WIELEMANS
Doyen d'honneur de la Brasserie Belge
Grand maître de la Chevalerie du Fourquet

EDITIONS • LA TECHNIQUE BELGE • BRUXELLES

The Memoirs of Jef Lambic, a very entertaining piece of 'lambic literature' which shows how lambic beers were a major part of Belgium's everyday life.

fermentation and blending themselves. Lambic beers account for 2.5 percent of the volume of beer produced in Belgium. (A list of lambic breweries and their products is presented in Appendix 1.) There are usually about a hundred products of the lambic kind on the market, though many are obtainable only on a very limited scale and in specialist cafés.

LAMBIC BREWERIES

Traditional lambic brewers offer products of the highest quality and safeguard old, artisanal lambic brewing techniques through their care and craftsmanship. Chief among them is the Cantillon brewery, 56-58 rue Gheude in Brussels, operated as a brewery and museum (Musée Bruxellois de la Gueuze) by Jean-Pierre and Claude Van Roy.

15

In 1937, Paul Cantillon, a beer merchant who blended his own lambics in Lambeek, built the small brewery with his two sons Robert and Marcel. The 1950s were glorious times, with father and sons brewing up to fifty five batches of lambic a year. But with the disappearance of the traditional café clientèle in the late 1960s, production slowed down.

Jean-Pierre Van Roy, a teacher turned brewmaster in 1969, understood the need to educate the public and develop a market of home consumers for his lambic beers. With his wife Claude, he created the Gueuze Museum in 1978 to preserve and promote the artisanal brewing of lambic beers and to protect their qualities and reputation. The live museum is a non-profit organization. It features the permanent display of brewing tools and equipment, the organization of tours, temporary exhibits and seminars, and extensive tastings of lambic products. The number of visitors steadily increases each year and reached 11,000 in 1989. Running the museum leaves little time for brewing, and production is down to a dozen batches of lambic a year. This is unfortunate because Cantillon brews are standards of lambic excellence.

Vandervelden produces some of the most authentic-tasting lambic beers in appropriately named Beersel. The Oud Beersel products of the brewery are very dry and quite sour. Girardin, in Sint-Ulriks-Kapelle, has been brewing since 1882 another traditional line of lambic products with outstanding qualities. When ordered in a Paris café, a bottle of Girardin gueuze or kriek is ceremoniously presented to the customer in a wine basket. Other brewers who make lambic beers by traditional methods include De Troch in Wambeek, Eylenbosh (formerly owned by Whitbread and just recently sold to the Maes group) in Schepdaal, Timmermans in Itterbeek, and Vander Linden in Halle.

The Lindemans brewery, installed on an eighteenth

century farm in Sint-Pieters-Leeuw, is the biggest exporter of lambic beer to the United States. Brewmaster René Lindemans combines traditional mashing and wort cooling with fermentation in large stainless-steel tanks, the addition of fruit syrups, filtration, and pasteurization. Lindemans kriek and framboise are well known to American beer connoisseurs and have captured the imagination of many American wine lovers.

The De Keersmaeker brewery in Kobbegem has brewed its famous *Mort Subite* line of lambic beers for 250 years. From 500,000 to 1 million gallons of *Mort Subite* are sold every year, mostly in Belgium and France. *Mort Subite* is French for sudden death. The name goes back to the beginning of this century, when brokers and bankers from the banking district in Brussels frequented the bistro La Cour Royale when the banks closed at midday. There they played a dice game called *pietjesbak* in which the loser (the dead) bought the beers. When the bell tolled, announcing the reopening of the banks, one last roll of the dice determined who would loose by "sudden death" and pick up the tab. The term also applied to a player having to vacate his spot during the game. In contradiction with the Belgian saying "from beer to bier," the *Mort Subite* brews, with an alcohol content on the low side, are not especially lethal.

A few breweries in West Flanders also have launched into the lambic side of the brewing market, despite their location away from the traditional zone for brewing lambic. Examples are the Bocker brewery in Courtrai and the Saint Louis brewery in Ingelmunster.

The Belle-Vue brewing group, founded in 1913 by Vanden Stock, is one of the largest brewing groups in Belgium. Over the past two decades, Belle-Vue has taken over several lambic breweries, including Brasseries Unies, De Keersmaeker, Brabrux, and De Neve. It brews some 75 percent of the total gueuze and kriek production in its units at Schepdaal, Molenbeek, Wolvertem, and Sint-Pieters-Leeuw. Belle-Vue uses the most advanced technology throughout most of the brewing process. Traditional techniques are still employed, however, for cooling the wort in open vats, fermenting in wooden casks, and blending different lambics. The Vanden Stock group is the leading brewer of filtered gueuze (especially under the Belle-Vue label), but it also brews and markets a small amount of gueuze, kriek, and framboise produced entirely in the traditional manner. An example is the unfiltered, refermented gueuze produced by De Neve. Belle-Vue received the Exportation Oscar from the Belgian Government in 1981 for selling gueuze, kriek, and framboise throughout the world.

The survival of lambic breweries is jeopardized by the very nature of their product. Lambic beers and their derivatives spend from several weeks to a few years in the brewery from the time they are brewed, to the time they are distributed in the trade. This means that large amounts of capital are tied up in casks and bottles. Even a small brewery may have between $100,000 and $300,000 tied up in maturing beer. Furthermore, the tax system is more stringent for lambic brewers. They must pay taxes on their product within a year after it is brewed. In short, since authentic lambic beers are not supposed to be sold before a year or two, lambic brewers end up lending money to the Belgian tax-collecting agencies. Some lambic brewers prefer to sell their lambic before it is mature to avoid losing money. In contrast, ale and lager brewers have thirty days to pay taxes on the products they make in two to four weeks. Another problem experienced by lambic brewers is facing retirement knowing that none of their offspring are willing to dedicate their lives to an old and arduous craft.

Cooling tun (*bac refroidissoir*). Belle-Vue Brewery.

LAMBIC CAFÉS AND BLENDERS

Belgian cafés, sometimes called *éstaminets*, are an important part of the lambic tradition. Not long ago, there was one café per 165 inhabitants in Belgium. A 1919 law banned spirit drinks from Belgian cafés, at the same time when restrictions on alcohol were being imposed in many parts of the world. This law, which is not always observed or enforced today, no doubt helped popularize strong beers such as gueuze, kriek, and framboise in Belgium. Sipping a few beers after work was, and still is a well-developed habit made possible by the large number and variety of cafés in Belgian cities and villages. Brussels has many estaminets with a wide selection of lambic products. The Art Nouveau café De Ultieme Hallucinatie, at 316 rue Royale, needs no translation from the Flemish. Le Spinnekop, at Place du Jardin aux Fleurs, offers a large selection of authentic gueuze and kriek.

The remarkably garish La Mort Subite, serving the

lambic beers of the same name, is located at 17 rue Montagne-aux-Herbes Potagères. The pub, which looks like an old railway station restaurant, has an interesting background. In 1926, Théophile Vossen was expropriated from the estaminet La Mort Subite (formerly La Cour Royale), which he had been running for a decade. Vossen moved to the rue Montagne-aux-Herbes and kept the same name for his café. Ironically, the new location for the Mort Subite café was next to a mortician's shop, which later went out of business. There, Vossen blended his own line of Mort Subite products. The tradition was carried on by his son Albert Vossen until 1962. The café now serves the Mort Subite products from the De Keersmaeker brewery.

The café La Bécasse, located at 11 rue Tabora, a small alley off the Grand Place, is most famous for its lambic doux. It also serves lambic beers brewed for the house by the Brabrux and De Neve breweries with delicious snacks like cream cheese toasts, bread with radishes and scallions, or charcuterie. Upon special request, one can also taste some authentic gueuze at the famous Toone puppet theater in Brussels, and at the Abbaye du Rouge Cloître in Auderghem. At the periphery of the city, other lambic cafés include Boendaalse at Steenweg 441; Le Miroir at Place Reine Astrid 24 in Jette; Moeder Lambic at Savoiestraat 68 in St. Gillis; and Le Jugement Dernier at Chaussée de Hacht in Schaarbeek. In Payottenland, each village has at least one café serving lambic beers. The Drie Fonteinen and Oude Pruim cafés in Beersel blend their own lambic.

Before World War I, there were about 300 beer merchants in Brussels who bought lambics, young and old, which they blended and refermented themselves to make gueuze. The considerable skills and experience required for such an exercise were a determinant factor in keeping up the quality of lambic beers over the years. Most merchants also owned an estaminet where they served their lambic, faro, and gueuze.

Today, there are about half a dozen companies called "blenders" that contract or buy lambic brews which they then ferment, mature, and blend in their own cellars. Frank Boon is a well-respected blender of lambic beers whose contribution to the renewed interest in lambic styles has been significant. He started blending his own products a few years back at the former De Vit brewery in Lembeek. His "Mariage Parfait" line of specialty blends is unique. Other blenders include De Koninck and De Troch, neither connected with the breweries of the same name, Moriau, Hanssens and Wets.

THE LAMBIC AND GUEUZE APPELLATIONS

The lambic and gueuze appellations are ill-protected. The gueuze drunk in Brussels is often different from exported gueuze. Since 1965, a royal order regulates the use of the lambic, gueuze, and so-called "gueuze lambic" appellations. These beers must be produced by spontaneous fermentation from at least 30 percent unmalted wheat; the exact proportions of malt and wheat must be entered in a register verifiable by the Ministry; the wort must have a gravity of at least 1.020 (5 degrees Plato); and the label on the bottle must show the name of the brewer and the location of the brewery, as well as list one of the three protected appellations. This order remains very vague, however, and leaves room for many different interpretations.

The royal order fails to address several points. There are no restrictions as to where lambic and gueuze can be brewed. Only the wheat fraction of the mash is defined, allowing some lambic brewers to substitute part of the malt fraction with lightly malted barley or even adjunct. The term spontaneous fermentation is not defined, which leads some brewers to artificially inoculate their wort to speed up the main fermentation. There are no limitations on the use of additives. There is no regulation of the kriek, framboise, cassis, pêche, and muscat appellations, and most brewers have long replaced whole fruit with syrups and artificial flavors. Likewise, while it is the blending of pure lambics of different ages (and residual fermentable extracts) that creates the natural carbonation of a true gueuze in the bottle, unfortunately, few breweries still use this method. Most artificially carbonate their beer or blend lambic with a top-fermented wheat beer that they have produced especially for this purpose. Another departure from tradition by some is the filtration (and sometimes pasteurization) of their gueuze before bottling.

It would be only fair of his Majesty King Baudouin to revise the order of 1965 and create distinct appellations for filtered, bulk-fermented gueuze and gueuze refermented in the bottle, and new ones for the many fruit derivatives of lambic. Gueuze and fruit lambics produced by fermentation in bulk should so state on the label to prevent them from competing unfairly with the more costly bottle-fermented lambics. The survival of small, traditional lambic brewers and their fine products may depend on it. Several proposals by small brewers to establish distinct appellations for bottle- and bulk-fermented lambics never made it to the Belgian Congress because of lobbying by influential big brewers. A recent attempt by the Association of Lambic Brewers to write a brochure for the promotion of lambic beers fell short because some members were not willing to have some of their "modern" brewing practices disclosed to the general public.

Why do spontaneous fermentation and ancient brewing practices still prevail in modern brewing only in the

Brussels area in Belgium? It is certain that the local microbial flora has a lot to do with it. The microorganisms that are required to successfully complete a lambic fermentation have found a niche perfectly suited for their ecological requirements in lambic breweries. Despite the tremendous amount of research performed at the University of Leuven and elsewhere, the lambic fermentation is not yet completely understood, and lambic beers remain an unresolved scientific issue in many ways. Also, blending houses keep the lambic tradition alive there. Blending became popular because the spontaneous fermentation of the lambic wort can have such unpredictable results. The last factor has to be the country and its people. Lambic beers are a very significant part of Belgium's brewing heritage and culture. To quote the beer writer Michael Jackson, "A nation divided between two different cultures (Flemish and Walloon) is inherently parochial and introspective, not always to its detriment." Belgium must protect lambic beers to remain the paradise of specialty beers, with more than 400 different kinds.

2

Sensory Profile

"The lambic family are not everybody's glass of beer, but no one with a keen interest in alcoholic drink would find them anything less than fascinating. In their "wildness" and unpredictibility, these are exciting brews. At their best, they are the meeting point between beer and wine. At their worst, they offer a taste of history." This statement from Michael Jackson sets the tone for introducing the sensory properties of lambic beers. The reaction of a first-time lambic drinker is inevitably one of surprise, sometimes shock. He/she finds characters that are not present in mainstream beers, such as excessive acidity, *Brettanomyces* character, wood aroma and astringency, little or no bitterness, and lots of fruit aroma. The ensuing relationship between the drinker and the beer is usually one of passionate love or hate. Lambic beers always generate extreme statements and are alternatively regarded as the best or the worst beers in the world by experts. Before tasting a glass of gueuze, kriek, or framboise, it is important to understand that some sensory attributes that are regarded as defects in other beers (volatile acidity, lactic acid, *Brettanomyces* character, etc.) are desirable in lambic beers.

The following table summarizes the terms that apply to describing lambic beers. The list differs somewhat from the "beer flavor wheel" because it accommodates descriptors unique to lambic and excludes descriptors that are appropriate only for other beers.

DESCRIPTORS OF THE SENSORY PROPERTIES OF LAMBIC BEERS

Appearance

Color (lambic & gueuze)	*Turbidity*
Golden yellow	Microbiological haze
Brownish yellow	Physical haze
Light amber	
Honey	*Foam*
Pale apricot	Stable - Collapsing
Color (fruit lambics)	
Orange	
Pink	
Ruby red	
Dark red	
Purple	

Aroma

Fruity* (fruit lambics)	*Floral*
Cherry	Linalool
Raspberry	
Black currant	*Estery*
Grapes/Muscat	Ethyl acetate
Peach	Ethyl lactate
Fruity*	*Winey/Vinous*
Apple	Wine
Apricot	Port
Red currant	Sherry
Melon	
Raisin	*Cidery*
'Artificial' fruit	Apple cider
Vegetative	*Grainy*
Aged hops	Malt
Hay/Straw	Barley
Tea	Wheat
Celery	
Artichoke	

Acetic
   Acetic acid (vinegarlike)

Woody
   Oak
   Pine
   Smoky
   Vanilla

Nutty
   Walnut
   Almond

Yeasty
   Saccharomyces

Sulfury
   DMS/Mercaptan
   Toasty

Animal
   Caprylic/goaty
   Mousy
   Leather

Other
   Earthy
   Moldy
   Soapy

Pungent
   Ethanol
   Spicy

Oxidized
   Acetaldehyde

Fruit pit
   Pits

Caramel
   Caramel
   Butterscotch
   Honey
   Chocolate

Brettanomyces
   Horse blanket
   Barn
   Sweat

Dairy
   Lactic/Yogurt
   Cheesy
   Butyric
   Rancid

Taste

Sourness
   Lactic acid

Sweetness
   Sweet - Dry

Bitterness
   Iso-alpha-acids

Mouthfeel

Body
   Thin - Thick
   Oily/Ropy

Astringency
   Smooth - Rough

Carbonation
   Flat - Gassy
   Bubbly
   Stingy

* Refers to one or several of the following: fresh fruit, cooked fruit, preserves, fruit skins.

LAMBICS AND FARO

A young or *fox* lambic is cloudy and still because the carbonation is not retained in the casks in which it has been fermented. The color is still close to the golden yellow of the wort, bordering on light amber as months go by.

The fermentation bouquet as we know it for ales or lagers has vanished, and the aroma includes vinegar notes from acetic acid and ethyl acetate, wine and cider scents, the beginning of a strong *Brettanomyces* character, and some almond.

The taste is usually very sour (lactic sourness) with some residual sweetness if the lambic is only one- to three-months old but quite dry otherwise. A very young lambic is not a well-balanced product because a few attributes predominate in an otherwise bland sensory background. After a year, lambic mellows, gaining in fruity aromas and gradually losing some of its sourness. The flavor becomes much more complex because many different compounds in moderate concentration make up the sensory properties of the beer.

Old lambic takes on a pinkish, sherrylike, amber color. It is completely devoid of carbon dioxide and very clear. The sour and oxidized flavor and the mellow, almost viscous mouthfeel are reminiscent of Château Chalon wines from the Jura region in France.

Faro is a very drinkable, moderately carbonated product. It retains most of the attributes of young lambic, but these are tempered with the caramel and raisin aromas and the sweet taste of the added dark candy sugar, bringing forth fruitiness at the onset and a complex aftertaste in the finish.

GUEUZE

The color of gueuze ranges from a golden yellow for a young gueuze to light amber for an old one. Apricotlike

Champion drinker. Unidentified Painter. Rijksmuseum, Amsterdam, Netherlands.

orange and sherrylike or honeylike brown also are common for gueuze. Authentic, bottle-fermented gueuze can have a high carbonation level and be very "gassy" like Champagne. The beer often gushes out of the bottle. A head of gueuze foam is midway between a normal white beer foam and a yellowish, sparkling wine foam. Bubbles are big and collapse quickly. This phenomenon is also enhanced by the relatively high serving temperature of 54 degrees F or higher (12 degrees C). The foam of bulk-fermented, filtered gueuze is similar to that of most ales.

Several kinds of aromas escape from a glass of gueuze. The volatile acidity is usually high and produces vinegarlike and goaty/cheesy aromas. Lots of fruit aromas are present, ranging from apple or melon to red currant and apricot. The *Brettanomyces* character comes through next, best described as horse blanket, leathery, barnlike, or horsey. It must have a reasonably low intensity not to border on the mousy or wet dog aromas and become objectionable to some drinkers. Ideally, it is balanced with the fruity notes, the wood and vanilla characters from the barrels, and the caramel aroma from the long wort boil. Nutty aromas and pine kernel notes are common. Some toasty notes (as in Champagne) from autolyzed yeast in the bottle may also be found. The unusual combination of aromas in gueuze often results in the use of terms such as cidery or winey to describe its overall aroma.

The taste of gueuze is sour, acidic, and sometimes harsh. Gueuze is usually devoid of bitterness. A few breweries have departed from that tradition, however, and produce gueuze that may be quite bitter. The sweetness depends on the amounts of residual sugar in the bottle. Gueuze ranges from being very dry for aged, bottle-fermented gueuze to distinctively sweet for mainstream bulk-fermented and filtered gueuze.

The mouthfeel of gueuze is unique: the high carbonation in the beer makes it foam inside the mouth and sting the tongue and palate. Traditional gueuze is usually astringent and thin because it has picked up tannins from the wheat and wood, and has a low real extract. Bulk-fermented gueuze has a much thicker and smoother mouthfeel.

The finish or aftertaste of gueuze usually combines a warming feeling from the high ethanol content with lingering, fruity and horsey aromas and a dry, puckery feeling from the sourness and astringency of the beer.

FRUIT LAMBICS

- Kriek -

A kriek displays a wide range of colors and flavors because of the many variations in the way it is processed. Authentic, traditional kriek combines the characteristics of bottle-fermented gueuze with the fresh fruit and pit aromas of the whole cherries and the residual sweetness of the young lambic added to the refermented, matured blend of lambics and cherries.

Kriek has a dark, ruby-red color with hints of purple and brown. The carbonation can be as erratic as that of gueuze, but the foam is usually more stable, with a smaller average bubble size. The dominant aroma should obviously be that of fresh cherry. Vanilla and caramel notes bridge the gap between the fruit character and the microbial aromas (volatile acidity and *Brettanomyces* character). The sourness is intense, but it is balanced by some residual sweetness. Compared to gueuze, kriek exhibits more astringency as a result of the cherries and pits.

- Framboise -

The color of framboise is ruby red, bordering on orange or brown depending on the age of the beer. The raspberry aroma is always very strong and masks part or most of the volatile acidity and *Brettanomyces* character. The aroma of the vanilla sometimes added to the brew blends nicely with the woody background. Traditional framboise is very dry, quite sour, and astringent. Mainstream framboise is on the smooth and sweet side.

- Cassis -

The cassis lambics on the market are designed to quench the thirst of young consumers. They are rather sweet and sour, with an overwhelming syruplike black currant aroma and virtually no *Brettanomyces* character.

- Pêche -
(patented by the Lindemans Brewery)

Pêche, commercialized under the name Pêcheresse, is a slightly turbid, apricot-orange beer, pasteurized, but only roughly filtered. The turbidity and the color come from the addition of whole fruit and peach concentrate to a blend of young lambics. The peach aroma that comes through resembles that of peach yogurt and peach preserves. It is slightly lactic and cooked or "artificial" as opposed to tasting like fresh fruit. It is so overwhelming that little volatile acidity or *Brettanomyces* character are perceived. Some woody/pit character is detectable, however, because of the use of wooden chips in the process. A good balance is achieved between sweetness and sourness, both being of medium intensity.

- Muscat -

Muscat or *druiven* is reminiscent of wine with some port and sherry notes. The color is pale violet/purple with shades of brown. The fresh-fruit aroma from the muscat should balance the volatile acidity. The wood character is pronounced, while the *Brettanomyces* aroma is kept low, yet detectable. Muscat lambic also exhibits astringency from the grapes.

3

Physical and Chemical Composition

Lambic, gueuze, and related beers are complex mixtures, the unique character of which depends on a few key components. Some of these components are derived from the unique raw materials used in their brewing process, e.g., unmalted wheat, aged hops, fruit, etc. Others arise from the unique brewing and fermentation processes themselves. In discussing lambic beers, it is essential to review their composition and compare it to that of other beers, as well as to examine the relationship between the composition of lambic beers and their sensory properties. In the table at the end of this chapter, the composition of lambic beers is contrasted with that of typical American lagers. Beer constituents are listed with their concentration range and the reference from which it was obtained. Additional data collected by the author is given without citation.

The specific gravity of lambic wort ranges from 1.048 to 1.055 (11.80 to 13.50 degrees Plato) for gueuze, and 1.040 to 1.072 (10 to 17.40 degrees Plato) for fruit lambics. A very high extraction of wort soluble solids is achieved during the long and complex lambic mashing process. The high original extract values found for some fruit lambics are caused by the addition of fruit or fruit syrups to the lambic.

Their contribution to the extract is added to that of the original wort.

Starting with the same specific gravity of 1.048 (12 degrees Plato), the real extract of gueuze and fruit lambics can be as low as 1.008 (2.2 degrees Plato), that is, half that of typical ales and lagers at 1.015 to 1.019 (3.7 to 4.8 degrees Plato). This is because of the higher degrees of attenuation and fermentation of lambic beers. The real degree of fermentation (RDF) of gueuze, which varies between 63 and 82 percent, exceeds by far that of American lagers, that are fermented only between 50 and 68 percent. The attenuation of sugars in gueuze, kriek, or framboise can be complete, leaving no sugars at all. This makes lambic beers attractive beverages for diabetic patients. Reducing sugars (expressed as maltose) range between traces and 0.8 percent in gueuze and between traces and 2 percent in fruit lambics. The high value of 2 percent sometimes occurs in the syrup-sweetened beers that undergo only a limited secondary fermentation and are quickly filtered and pasteurized. These beers have a pronounced sweet taste.

Virtually no dextrins are found in gueuze and fruit lambics, provided they have gone through the traditional primary fermentation in casks and secondary fermentation in the bottle. Otherwise, some dextrins may remain in the beer from unmalted wheat or lightly malted barley that give worts higher in dextrin than fully malted barley. The low level of dextrins in authentic lambics is one of the reasons why their mouthfeel is characterized as being rather "thin."

A wide range of alcohol concentrations is found in lambic products. Faro averages 3.5 percent ethanol by volume (2.8 percent w/w). A young lambic contains about 4.5 percent v/v (3.6 percent w/w) ethanol. The alcoholic content of gueuze varies from 5.3 to 6.2 percent v/v (4.2 percent to 5 percent w/w). That of fruit lambics can be slightly higher, up to 6.5 percent v/v (5.2 percent w/w) because of the additional fermentable extract contributed by the fruit. These ethanol concentrations are reached from a 12 to 13 degrees Plato original extract because of the high attenuation observed in lambic and gueuze produced the traditional way. However, to produce kriek or framboise, some brewers mix fruit syrups and young lambic and stop the fermentation by pasteurizing shortly thereafter. Beers produced that way are much lower in ethanol, down to 3.7 percent v/v (2.9 percent w/w), and very sweet. To resolve the confusion about the alcohol content in their beers, some producers put the ethanol by volume on the label.

An accurate determination of the ethanol concentration is required because, in Belgium, as in most brewing countries, the excise tax is levied on the measured alcoholic content of the beer. The unit of taxation is the *hectolitre-degré* (hL-degré). One hL-degré corresponds to one hectoliter of beer with 1 percent ethanol by volume (0.79 percent w/w). For example, starting with 50.3 barrels (60 hL) of lambic wort, Jean-Pierre Van Roy at the Cantillon Brewery produces 43.6 barrels (52 hL) of gueuze at 6 percent ethanol v/v (4.8 percent w/w) that is, $52 \times 6 = 312$ taxable hL-degrés. The excise tax currently runs at 67 Belgian Francs ($1.80 U.S.) per hL-degré.

Most lambic beers get their calories from the ethanol they contain and not from their residual extract, which is very low. They have a slightly higher caloric value than American lagers. Some fruit lambics, not fermented dry and pasteurized, can be much more caloric as a result of their high residual sugar.

The level of acetaldehyde, the oxidation product of ethanol, is surprisingly low in lambic beers (2.5 to 8.2 mg/L), considering the potential for oxidation of the lambic in wooden casks or during transfer operations.

35

All beers of the lambic style are acetic in smell and sour in taste because they contain high levels of organic acids. Their total acidity is three to eight times that of American lagers. The pH of lambic ranges from 3.4 for "hard" lambic, that is, lambic infected with acetic acid bacteria, to 3.9 for "soft" lambic. "Ropy" lambics that contain a high density of *Pediococcus* have a pH of about 3.5. The pH of gueuze, kriek, and framboise is even lower, ranging from 3.32 to 3.51 for gueuze, and 3.30 to 3.51 for fruit lambics. This is due to further microbial activity resulting in the production of acetic and lactic acids, and/or to the acidity of the fruits (usually sour varieties) macerated in kriek, framboise, pêche, and cassis. In comparison, the pH of American lagers is between 3.8 and 4.7.

The concentration of acetic acid in gueuze may be as high as 1,200 mg/L. On average, it is generally higher in refermented gueuze than in filtered gueuze. Most of the acetic acid is produced early in the lambic fermentation. In lambic casks infected with acetic acid bacteria, it may reach 4,000 mg/L. These lambics have excessive pungent and vinegar characters, and they are eventually used for blending. Some acetic acid is lost to evaporation and esterification, by which it is converted to ethyl acetate.

With regard to lactic acid, the evolution of the concentration over time differs from that of acetic acid. About 800 mg/L is found in lambic after the first month of fermentation. The concentration of lactic acid then rises to values of 2,000 to 4,000 mg/L in the next six to eight months. Exceptionally, concentrations of 10,000 mg/L and up have been measured in ropy lambics heavily infected with *Pediococcus* strains. In gueuze, kriek, and framboise, the concentration of lactic acid may be as high as 6,300 mg/L. More common values, however, are 1,500 to 3,500 mg/L. On average, it is higher in refermented gueuze than in

Checking the clarity of the wort during run off. Cantillon Brewery.

filtered gueuze. The level of lactic acid in lambic beers is the main determinant of their low pH and their sourness. In comparison, other beers usually contain 55 to 145 mg/L of acetic acid and 40 to 150 mg/L of lactic acid, unless they have been infected.

Propionic, isobutyric, and butyric acids are also found at higher concentrations in lambic beers causing dairy, cheesy flavors. Butyric acid averages 4 and 5 mg/L in filtered and refermented gueuze, respectively, compared to only 0.6 mg/L in other beers.

Interestingly, malic acid is found in some fruit lambics, at concentrations as high as 6,600 mg/L. There is virtually no malic acid in any of the ingredients normally used to make beer. Indeed, the concentration range for ales and lagers is 15 to 105 mg/L. Most fruits and fruit syrups, however, contain high amounts of malic acid. In wine, malic acid from grapes can be converted to lactic acid through the malolactic fermentation, which is effected by lactic acid bacteria of the *Lactobacillus* or *Leuconostoc* genera. Given time and the proper conditions of temperature and pH, it is likely that fruit lambics also can undergo a malolactic fermentation because they contain *Pediococcus* or *Lactobacillus* bacteria that can effect the malolactic fermentation. Examining the malic acid concentration in kriek, framboise, and other fruit lambics might therefore be a good way to assess how long the beer was refermented and matured after addition of the fruit.

The higher fatty acid (HFA) profile of lambic and gueuze differs from that of other beers. HFAs have an impact on foam structure and flavor—either directly or indirectly—through the formation of esters. These acids usually occur in beer in total amounts of 10 to 20 mg/L. While the total HFA content of lambic and gueuze is only slightly higher (14 to 36 mg/L), these beers have two or three times more caprylic (C_8) and capric (C_{10}) acids than do other beers. This is especially true of refermented gueuze. The additive flavor effect of the C_6-C_{12} fatty acids in lambic and gueuze often exceeds their combined flavor threshold of about 10 mg/L and may result in a goaty or "caprylic" flavor.

The concentrations of higher alcohols (fusel oils) in lambics are not different from those found in ales or lagers. Filtered gueuze usually has higher levels of propanol than does refermented gueuze. During the extensive storage of bottled lambic beers, higher alcohols can be oxidized to aldehydes by melanoidins. Aldehydes affect the flavor of the beer (giving it apple, oxidized characters), whereas melanoidins give it a darker color and thicker, more viscous mouthfeel.

With respect to esters, very large differences are observed between lambic or gueuze and other beers. Much of the peculiar fruity flavor of gueuze is a result of its ester composition. The volatile terpenes that make up most of the essential hop oils are not a factor in lambic beers because old hops are used in the brewing process. The average concentration of ethyl acetate is much higher, ranging from 12 to 31 mg/L in lambic, 33 to 68 mg/L in filtered gueuze, and 61 to 167 mg/L in refermented gueuze (Van Oevelen *et al.*; 1976). In the case of hard lambic, (again, lambic infected with acetic acid bacteria), the concentration of ethyl acetate may be as high as 540 mg/L. The normal range in American ales and lagers is 6-23 mg/L.

The acetic, vinegarlike odor of lambics is a result of both acetic acid and ethyl acetate. These two compounds are usually produced simultaneously and proportionately, but because ethyl acetate has a lower detection threshold, it contributes more than acetic acid to the acetic smell of lambic beers. Most striking is the difference in ethyl lactate concentration between lambics and other beers. Whereas ethyl lactate averages only 0.1 mg/L in other beers, it ranges from 22 to 140 mg/L in lambic, 107 to 143 mg/L in filtered gueuze, and 361 to 483 mg/L in refermented gueuze. On the other hand, the concentration of iso-amyl acetate (<0.1 to 0.19 mg/L in lambic and 0.1 to 5.0 mg/L in gueuze) is usually lower than that found in other beers (0.7 to 3.3 mg/L). Gueuze also is characterized by a relatively low content of phenethyl acetate. High amounts of the fatty acid esters ethyl caprylate (0.16 to 0.59 mg/L) and ethyl caprate (0.07 to 0.28 mg/L) also are found in lambic and gueuze. Since ethyl caprate is almost absent in other beers, it is likely to be a major component of the aroma of lambic and gueuze (Spaepen et al.; 1979).

Other volatile compounds such as diacetyl or dimethyl sulfide (DMS) are found in lambic beers at concentrations similar to those observed for ales and lagers. These compounds are usually produced early in the lambic fermentation and evaporate to some extent during maturation (Van Oevelen *et al.;* 1978). A high diacetyl content in lambic beers usually indicates strong *Pediococcus* activity or oxidation problems.

The unique contribution of *Brettanomyces* to the aroma of lambic and gueuze is a result of not only the high amounts of ethyl acetate and ethyl lactate it produces, but also the formation of some tetrahydropyridines and volatile phenols (Craig and Heresztyn; 1984; Heresztyn; 1986 a, b). The tetrahydropyridines likely are responsible for the horsey, leathery aroma of lambic beers, and the volatile phenols probably account for some of the spicy, smokelike, or clovelike odors sometimes found in lambic and gueuze.

BITTERNESS

Bitterness units (BUs), as determined by the ASBC method of extraction with isooctane followed by measurement of the absorbance of the extract at 275 nanometers (nm) are supposed to express the bitter taste of beer satisfactorily, regardless of whether the beer was made with fresh or old hops. [In this method, degased, acidified beer (10 mL) is extracted with isooctane (20 ml) by agitating the mixture for fifteen minutes. The absorbance of the isooctane layer is then read at 275 nm in a spectrophotometer. BUs are equal to fifty times absorbance of the isooctane extracts—the bitter principles (mostly iso-alpha acids) from the beer. These principles absorb light at 275 nm.] Lambic beers have roughly the same amount of BUs (11.7 to 22.4) as American lagers (10 to 23), and yet they taste much less bitter. There are two explanations for this discrepancy. The hopping rate of lambic wort is much higher than that of lager wort, but all the alpha- and beta-acids in the old hops used for lambic are oxidized. Although they are extracted by the isooctane, they do not absorb as well at 275 nanometers as the iso-alpha-acids of lager beers. Yet, they still absorb some, and since there is more of them, they probably account for the 12 to 23 measured BUs. Also, the high acidity in gueuze and the residual sweetness in some fruit lambics probably mask what little bitterness might be present in these beers. Some brewers use hops that have not been thoroughly aged (and oxidized) and produce the few bitter lambics on the market.

CARBONATION

The carbon dioxide content of lambic beers varies widely, especially in bottle-fermented gueuze. A high CO_2 level combined with the presence of oxidative yeasts in the bottle can cause gushing upon opening. Bulk-fermented and filtered products typically have a slightly lower CO_2 content (2.0 to 2.4 volumes) than do mainstream ales and lagers (2.4 to 2.8 volumes).

CLARITY

Some lambic beers are hazy because they have not been through a polish filtration or because they have been bottle-conditioned. In such cases, a biological haze made of viable yeasts and bacteria is sometimes visible, even without disturbance of the sediment at the bottom. In addition, some lambic beers might throw a chill haze because of their protein and polyphenol content. The incidence of nonbiological haze, however, is lower than with other beers. This is because the total protein content (sediment not included) of lambic beers is usually low. The measurement of total protein in beer using the Bradford method based on the staining of proteins with Coomassie Brilliant Blue gives concentrations of 42 to 55 mg/L for gueuze, 30 to 69 mg/L for fruit lambics, *versus* 95 to 147 mg/L for commercial lagers. This is an interesting phenomenon because starting with raw ingredients (notably wheat) higher in protein than those used by lager brewers, the lambic brewer makes a product with a lower level of residual, undegraded protein. The rationale for this difference is found in the extensive boiling of the wort and the long fermentation and maturation processes. Basic aminoacids (arginine and lysine) from the wort are almost completely depleted by enteric bacteria during the first month of the lambic fermentation. From 100 mg/L in the original wort, their concentration drops to 10 mg/L (Verachtert; 1983). In contrast, the average concentration of essential aminoacids valine, leucine, isoleucine, methionine, phenylalanine, lysine, threonine, and histidine is four times higher in refermented gueuze than in other beers (Verachtert; 1983). This is probably a result of the release of aminoacids from autolyzed yeasts or bacteria into the beer.

PHENOLIC COMPOUNDS

The phenolic compounds in lambic beers range from relatively simple compounds produced by the wheat and malt grains (and the fruits in fruit lambics) to complex tannin-type substances extracted from the wood of the casks (and the pits, seeds, and skins in fruit lambics) during fermentation and aging. Although phenol extraction from the wood is limited because old, used casks house the lambic fermentations, it is still significant because of the very long time the lambics spend in these casks (sometimes up to three years). Phenols are important because they determine the fruit lambics' color (anthocyanins), impart a woody flavor (volatile phenols) and an astringent mouthfeel (tannins), serve as a reservoir for oxygen reduction, and are a source of browning substrate. The astringency of lambic tannins is further increased by the very low pH of the beer. This is because at low pH, tannins exist in a molecular configuration that is more astringent. The total phenol concentration of gueuze (560 to 600 mg/L) is twice that of American lagers (245 to 340 mg/L). Fruit lambics contain even more phenols, ranging from 600 to 960 mg/L.

COLOR

Lambic beers exhibit a wide array of colors, some of which are most unusual for beer. Accepted methods of beer color measurement (degrees EBC, Lovibond, or SRM) are inappropriate in the case of fruit lambics, the color of which is obviously determined almost exclusively by the fruit. The maceration of fruits in the lambic usually modifies the hue (pink, red, purple, brown, or orange) and the saturation of color by increasing the concentration of anthocyanins.

The color of lambic and gueuze can be examined with traditional methods. Generally, it varies from golden yellow for young lambic to light amber for gueuze. Gueuze ranges from 7 to 10 degrees Lovibond (8 to 13 degrees SRM). In comparison, American lagers have a lighter color, ranging from 2 to 4 degrees Lovibond (2 to 5 degrees SRM). The unmalted wheat used in the lambic mash has little effect on color, and the malt comprising the rest of the grist is pale. Color formation takes place during the very extensive boiling of the wort through Maillard reactions between amines and sugars yielding melanoidins and caramel. Additional color is picked up in the casks (directly from the wood or from browning — oxidation — reactions) during fermentation and maturation of the lambic.

Figures 1 and 2 show the HPLC (high performance liquid chromatography) profiles of selected lambic beers. These profiles provide a good picture of their composition and give some insight on the brewing practices used to make them. They show sugars, low-molecular-weight dextrins, organic acids, and ethanol. The size of the peak corresponding to a given compound is directly proportional to the concentration of that compound in the beer. The value listed next to each peak indicates the retention time in minutes of the corresponding compound(s): salts' buffer (2.3); malic acid (2.7); lactic acid (2.9); acetic acid (3.2); glucose (3.2); maltose (3.7); maltotriose — double-peak — (4.6, 5.0); maltotetraose — double-peak — (5.7, 6.2); and ethanol (6.8). Retention times may vary slightly due to pressure changes in the column between runs.

Figure 1, a, shows the profile of gueuze refermented in the bottle made the traditional way from a mixture of young and old lambics. Lactic and acetic acids peaks are very high, there is virtually no glucose and maltose, and some dextrins are left (probably from wheat). The high ethanol indicates a high original extract or a high degree of fermentation.

Figure 1, b, shows the profile of gueuze refermented in the bottle made with young lambics with insufficient fermentation and maturation. Lactic and acetic acid peaks are average, and fairly significant amounts of carbohydrates (glucose, maltose, maltotriose, maltotetraose, DP6, and DP7) are left. There is correspondingly little ethanol.

Figure 2, a, shows the profile of kriek produced the traditional way with maceration of whole fruits, lengthy fermentation and maturation in casks, and bottle-conditioning. No malic acid is left from the fruit, there are high amounts of lactic and acetic acids, and virtually no residual sugars and dextrins remain. Ethanol is very high, though some of it was probably lost in casks by evaporation.

Figure 2, b, shows kriek made with cherry concentrate, filtered and pasteurized after limited fermentation and aging. High malic acid from the concentrate is present, there are glucose/fructose peaks, with some maltose and low ethanol.

Figure 2, c, shows cassis made with black currant concentrate or cream (which contains ethanol), filtered and pasteurized after short fermentation and aging; it could contain top-fermented beer. High malic acid remains with

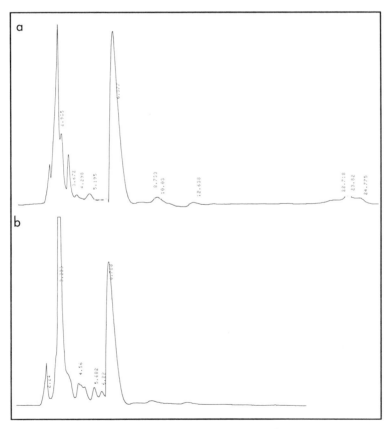

Figure 1. HPLC profiles of two commercial gueuzes. Each peak represents one or more compounds. Values indicate retention times for each peak.

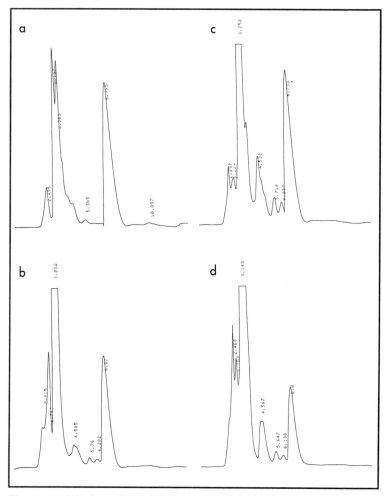

Figure 2. HPLC profiles of four commercial fruit lambics. Each peak represents one or more compounds. Values indicate retention times for each peak.

high glucose/fructose and maltose, and some maltotriose and maltotetraose. There is a fairly high amount of ethanol.

Figure 2, d, shows pêche produced from peach syrup. Malic acid is high, and there is glucose and fructose, some maltose, and little ethanol.

COMPOSITION TABLE

PARAMETER	AMERICAN LAGERS

Apparent extract (% w/w)

0.091–3.352 (gueuze)	2.000–3.100
0.615–8.502 (fruit)	

Real extract (% w/w) (S.G.)

4.479 (1.0176) (soft lambic)[a]	3.700–4.800
3.750 (1.0147) (hard lambic)[a]	
(1.0145–1.0189)	
4.730 (1.0186) (ropy lambic)[a]	
2.230–5.258 (1.0087–1.0207) (gueuze)	
2.240 (1.0088) (gueuze)[b]	
2.324–9.791 (1.0091–1.0392) (fruit)	

Original Extract (% w/w) (S.G.)

11.83–13.43 (1.0477–1.0544) (gueuze)	11.00–12.50
12.10 (1.0488) (gueuze)[b]	
(1.0442–1.0505)	
12.21 (1.0493) (gueuze)[c]	
10.01–17.37 (1.0401–1.0714) (fruit)	

Ethanol (% w/w)

4.25–4.95 (gueuze)	3.50–4.20
5.20 (gueuze)[b]	
4.05 (gueuze)[c]	
2.92–4.65 (fruit)	

Ethanol (% v/v)

4.50 (lambic)[d]	4.20–5.00
3.50 (faro)[d]	
5.34–6.20 (gueuze)	
5.50 (gueuze)[d]	
5.30–8.30 (gueuze)[e]	
3.68–5.84 (fruit)	
6.00 (fruit)[d]	

PARAMETER	AMERICAN LAGERS

Apparent Degree of Fermentation (%)

75.04–99.23 (gueuze)	65.00–75.00
44.61–93.86 (fruit)	

Real Degree of Fermentation (%)

62.55–82.09 (gueuze)	50.00–68.00
38.14–77.72 (fruit)	

Reducing Sugars (% w/v as maltose)

Traces–0.80 (gueuze)	0.40–0.90
0.25 (gueuze)[b]	
Traces–2.00 (fruit)	

Calories (Cal/100 mL)

44.5 (gueuze)[c]	29.0–32.0

Bitterness Units (BUs)

11.70–22.35 (gueuze)	10.00–23.00
15.35–21.35 (fruit)	

Color (Degrees Lovibond)

7.0–10.0 (gueuze)	2.0–4.0

Color (Degrees S.R.M.)

8.0–13.0 (gueuze)	2.0–5.0

Total Proteins (mg/L, Bradford method)

42.0–55.0 (gueuze)	95.0–147.0
30.0–69.0 (fruit)	

Total Phenols (mg/L gallic acid equivalents)

564–603 (gueuze)	245–340
596–962 (fruit)	

Composition Table

PARAMETER   AMERICAN LAGERS

Total Acidity (% as lactic acid)
0.62–1.10 (gueuze)   0.09–0.20
0.78–1.71 (fruit)

pH
3.90 (soft lambic)[a]   3.80–4.70
3.40 (hard lambic)[a]
3.50 (ropy lambic)[a]
3.32–3.51 (gueuze)
3.25–3.40 (ref. gueuze)[a]
3.20–3.45 (fil. gueuze)[a]
3.30–3.51 (fruit)

Acetic acid (mg/L)
766 (soft lambic)[a]   55–145
3944 (hard lambic)[a]
530 (ropy lambic)[a]
656–1210 (ref. gueuze)[a]
538–1177 (fil. gueuze)[a]

Lactic acid (mg/L)
492 (soft lambic)[a]   40–150
3677 (hard lambic)[a]
13446 (ropy lambic)[a]
1441–3820 (gueuze)
1890–3434 (ref. gueuze)[a]
2071–2890 (fil. gueuze)[a]
806–6276 (fruit)

Malic acid (mg/L)
100–6620 (fruit)   15–105

Butyric acid (mg/L) rancid, sour milk
3.4–6.0 (ref. gueuze)[a]   0.4–0.7
2.0–6.3 (fil. gueuze)[a]

49

PARAMETER	AMERICAN LAGERS

Propionic acid (mg/L) cheesy

1.0–52.5 (ref. gueuze)[a]	N. A.
1.3–5.8 (fil. gueuze)[a]	

Isobutyric acid (mg/L) sweaty

3.5–7.0 (ref. gueuze)[a]	2.5–3.5
1.1–2.5 (fil. gueuze)[a]	

Caproic (C_6) acid (mg/L) goaty

3.96–9.79 (ref. gueuze)[g]	3.10–5.80*
4.28–10.55 (fil. gueuze)[g]	

Caprylic (C_8) acid (mg/L) goaty

12.40–21.85 (ref. gueuze)[f]	6.30–12.30*
7.15–13.04 (ref. gueuze)[g]	
6.76–18.79 (fil. gueuze)[g]	

Capric (C_{10}) acid (mg/L) goaty

2.30–3.90 (ref. gueuze)[f]	0.40–1.80*
1.06–3.56 (ref. gueuze)[g]	
1.51–4.62 (fil. gueuze)[g]	

Propanol (mg/L) fusel or fusel oils

9.2 (soft lambic)[a]	5.40
8.7 (hard lambic)[a]	
5.0 (ropy lambic)[a]	
17.1 (lambic)[h]	
9.3–23.7 (ref. gueuze)[a]	
17.6–38.6 (fil. gueuze)[a]	

Butanol (mg/L) fusel or fusel oils

<0.1 (soft, hard, ropy lambic)[a]	N. A.
0.1–0.5 (ref. gueuze)[a]	
0.1–0.4 (fil. gueuze)[a]	

PARAMETER	AMERICAN LAGERS

Isobutanol (mg/L) fusel or fusel oils

18.8 (soft lambic)[a]	N. A.
15.4 (hard lambic)[a]	
7.0 (ropy lambic)[a]	
20.5 (lambic)[h]	
16.3–21.0 (ref. gueuze)[a]	
14.0–18.0 (fil. gueuze)[a]	
24.2 (gueuze)[h]	

Isoamyl alcohol (mg/L) fusel or fusel oils

57.9 (soft lambic)[a]	N. A.
53.1 (hard lambic)[a]	
39.5 (ropy lambic)[a]	
31.0 (lambic)[h]	
44.3–59.2 (ref. gueuze)[a]	
42.5–67.1 (fil. gueuze)[a]	
44.0 (gueuze)[h]	

D-Amyl alcohol (mg/L) fusel or fusel oils

15.6 (soft lambic)[a]	N. A.
11.4 (hard lambic)[a]	
9.0 (ropy lambic)[a]	
11.7–19.7 (ref. gueuze)[a]	
13.9–19.8 (fil. gueuze)[a]	

Phenethyl alcohol (mg/L) rose

45.8 (soft lambic)[a]	19.5
38.1 (hard lambic)[a]	
64.0 (ropy lambic)[a]	
20.7–54.0 (ref. gueuze)[a]	
32.0–42.0 (fil. gueuze)[a]	

Lambic

PARAMETER	AMERICAN LAGERS

Ethyl acetate (mg/L) solventlike, vinegary

30.1 (soft lambic)[a]   8.0–23.0
539.8 (hard lambic)[a]
12.2 (ropy lambic)[a]
31.4 (lambic)[h]
95.0 (gueuze)[h]
96.3 (gueuze)[i]
60.9–167.0 (ref. gueuze)[a]
33.4–67.6 (fil. gueuze)[a]

Ethyl lactate (mg/L) fruity, ethereal

21.9 (soft lambic)[a]   0.0–0.1
140.3 (hard lambic)[a]
79.0 (ropy lambic)[a]
407.0 (gueuze)[i]
361.0–483.0 (ref. gueuze)[a]
107.0–143.0 (fil. gueuze)[a]

Isoamyl acetate (mg/L) banana

<0.1 (soft, hard, ropy lambics)[a]   0.70–3.30
0.19 (lambic)[h]
0.28 (gueuze)[h]
0.50 (gueuze)[i]
0.10–4.90 (ref. gueuze)[a]
0.60–5.00 (fil. gueuze)[a]

Ethyl caproate (mg/L) fruity, estery, winey

0.19 (ref. gueuze)[f]   0.14–0.28*
0.17–0.35 (ref. gueuze)[g]
0.14–0.31 (fil. gueuze)[g]

Ethyl caprylate (mg/L) fruity, estery, winey

0.49 (ref. gueuze)[f]   0.17–0.22*
0.38–0.59 (ref. gueuze)[g]
0.16–0.51 (fil. gueuze)[g]

52

PARAMETER	AMERICAN LAGERS

Ethyl caprate (mg/L) fruity, estery, winey

0.26 (ref. gueuze)[f]	0
0.15–0.28 (ref. gueuze)[g]	
0.07–0.10 (fil. gueuze)[g]	

Phenethyl acetate (mg/L) honey or rose

0.09 (ref. gueuze)[f]	0.40–0.60
0.05–0.15 (ref. gueuze)[g]	
0.15–0.53 (fil. gueuze)[g]	

Acetaldehyde (mg/L)

2.5–8.2 (ref. gueuze)[a]	2.0–18.0
3.0–5.5 (fil. gueuze)[a]	

Dimethyl sulfide (mg/L)

100 (lambic)[j]	59–106

Diacetyl (mg/L)

45 (lambic)[j]	20–200

* Belgian lagers
N. A. Not available

a. Van Oevelen et al.; 1976
b. Plevoets and Van Ginderachter; 1988
c. Vanbelle et al.; 1972
d. Jackson; 1988
e. Berger and Duboë–Laurence; 1985
f. Spaepen et al.; 1978
g. Spaepen et al.; 1979
h. De Keersmaeker; 1974
i. Spaepen and Verachtert; 1982
j. Van Oevelen et al.; 1978

4

The Lambic
Brewing Process

INGREDIENTS

- Malt -

The malt used to brew lambic beers is pale, highly enzymic malt made mostly from spring-sown, two-row barley grown in Europe. Examples of varieties are Plaisant and Triumph. Germination is conducted until the rootlets reach half an inch in length. The malt is dried rather slowly and is never kilned (cured). So-called "wind-malts" sometimes find some use in lambic brewing: they are prepared in Belgium by thinly spreading green malt from six-row barley on screens in special lofts, and leaving it to dry. The resulting material supposedly has a very high enzyme content. The largest lambic brewery uses mostly French winter barley malted under contract by Belgian maltsters.

- Wheat -

The use of a high percentage of raw (unmalted) wheat in their mash (up to 40 percent) sets lambic brewers apart from other brewers. The germination of wheat is a difficult operation to conduct on an industrial scale because of its complex chemical composition. This is why unmalted wheat has traditionally been used to brew lambic beers. In consequence, the requirements for gelatinizing and converting the starch contained in the wheat kernel result in special mashing practices. Wheat selected for brewing lambic beers is usually a "soft" variety (as opposed to "hard" or "durum" varieties), more often white than red, having a "mealy" or "floury" endosperm. Traditional brewers use local varieties like the "Petit Roux du Brabant."

All the wheat supply used in lambic beers comes from Belgium. Compared to barley, wheat contains more starch and protein and less cellulose (fiber) and lipids. A high protein content in a cereal is not a desirable feature for brewing. Whereas wheat is regarded as a cereal with a high nitrogen (and protein) content, the soft, white varieties used in lambic brewing remain reasonably low in total nitrogen, with values ranging between 1.8 and 2.1 percent of the grain dry weight. In comparison, the total nitrogen in barley is between 1.5 and 1.8 percent. Wheat also contributes some bitterness and astringency to lambic beers and lowers their chill stability. One problem associated with the use of soft, white wheat is that it does not lauter as well as hard, red wheat. The lambic mash indeed is much more gummy in appearance than regular malt mashes. Ideally, the moisture of the wheat at milling should be between 15 and 17 percent. A lower moisture makes the grain harder, although it facilitates its storage.

Another part of the wheat plant, the chaff or *kaf,* may also find a use in lambic brewing as a filter aid. When wheat is harvested, the kernels are separated from their envelopes or chaff, which is a light material made of cellulose and fiber. Unlike barley kernels, wheat kernels do not have a husk. In a mash with up to 40 percent wheat, there is not enough husk material (only the husks from the 60 percent barley malt) to ensure proper lautering. This is why wheat chaff is sometimes used by brewers to improve the lautering of lambic worts. This material contains virtually no soluble substances. However, when it is boiled with part of the mash during a decoction or simply in contact with hot sparging water, it can contribute a yellow color and a marked strawlike odor to the wort. These sensory characteristics used to be part of the lambic bouquet. Now, however, very few lambic brewers use wheat chaff.

Wheat is sometimes replaced in part by rice or corn in lambic mashes. The resulting worts seem to ferment and mature faster, but they lose some of the characteristic flavor notes imparted by wheat. Beers in which wheat has been substituted by rice or corn do not deserve the lambic appellation. They are not true to type, as easily detected by taste.

Sacks of wheat and barley malt, and bags of aged hops stored in the loft. Cantillon Brewery.

One lambic brewer, who makes the famous Mort Subite, uses a rye grain called *tarwe* instead of, or in combination with wheat.

- Water -

Some brewing centers of the world have become renowned for the special quality of their water, which truly contributes to the unique quality of the beers they produce. Thus, Burton-on-Trent is famous for its strong pale ale, London and Dublin for their dark ales, Munich for its dark lagers, and Plzên for its pale lagers. Such is not the case in Brussels and its surroundings. Most lambic brewers use well water that does not have any outstanding qualities. Some brewers add calcium carbonate or calcium sulfate to adjust the hardness of the water. The lambic breweries located in Brussels use city and well water. The city water has a high hardness, which is treated by softening it or by scrubbing the kettle every once in a while, depending on the size and means of the brewery. The largest lambic brewery, located in Brussels, consumes 85 percent ground water (for brewing purposes) and 15 percent city water (for cleaning purposes).

- Hops -

The lambic brewer uses aged (*surannés*) hops that have lost most, if not all of their bittering properties. Traditionally, these hops came from the Alost and Poperinhge regions in Belgium. Now, Belgium has only about 2,000 acres (800 hectares) of hops under cultivation. These hops have been replaced in lambic beers by hops from the Kent region in England. Interestingly, the English hop industry dates back to the Middle Ages when Flemish (Belgian) weavers took hops across the Channel. The number of hop varieties grown commercially today in England exceeds that of any other country. The most commonly used varieties are Brewers Gold, Northern Brewer, Bramling Cross, Fuggles, and to a lesser extent, Bullion and Goldings. Hops from Alsace and central Europe generally are not recommended for lambic beers because with age, their bitterness turns into an acridity that is undesirable. Yet a significant amount of Saaz and Hallertau hops are used by the large lambic breweries.

Only whole hops are used because there is no industry to convert aged hops into pellets. The hops are aged for one to three years. From a biochemical point of view, aging hops results in their oxidation. Upon oxidation, alpha-acids, the main bittering acids in hops, lose their bittering ability. On the other hand, beta-acids, which are not bitter, gain bittering power upon oxidation. The amount of bitter beta-acid oxidation products is not sufficient, however, to compensate for the loss of alpha-acids, and the bittering potential decreases. After being aged (oxidized) for two or three years, hops have lost virtually all their bittering power. Old hops usually develop an unpleasant cheesy aroma as a result of oxidation of the hop resins. The volatile acids responsible for that cheesy aroma are expelled during wort boiling, which is particularly long and vigorous for lambic wort. The preservative value of hops is not lost upon aging, however, and remains the primary reason for their use in lambic brewing, since the hops contribute virtually no aroma (long boil) and no bitterness (aged hops).

BREWING OPERATIONS

- Milling -

First, the wheat is milled. Wheat, in contrast to most barley varieties, is a naked grain (no husk) with a deep crease running along its ventral side, which complicates the milling process. It is also much harder than barley malt, having not been malted. The main objective in milling the wheat is to separate the starchy endosperm both from the embryo and the bran (pericarp, testa and aleurone layer). A good conversion of the wheat starch during mashing also depends on the adequate disruption of the cell walls in the endosperm. As a result, a rather fine grist is wanted.

Traditionally, hammer-milling has been the method of choice for crushing wheat, but mostly roller mills are found in lambic breweries because they can be used to mill both wheat and malt. The gap settings between the rollers simply are increased from 0.04 to 0.06 inches for wheat and malt milling (respectively). The malt is coarse-ground to break the endosperm and to keep the husk intact. The kinds of mills (*concasseur*) found in lambic breweries vary just as much as they do in the lager or ale brewing industries. The smallest breweries use simple two- or four-roll mills, while the larger breweries use more complex ones.

- Mashing -

Typically, 35 percent wheat and 65 percent barley malt make up the grist for a lambic brew. Sometimes, the wheat is replaced with corn or rice, but as mentioned previously, the resulting lambic is of lower quality. Three types of beers can be produced from this typical brew: lambic, faro and mars beer depending on the specific gravity of the wort. Mashing takes place in a traditional mash tun (*cuve matière*) with a slotted false bottom to draw the wort. The mash tun is equipped with a system of rotating rakes for mixing the mash. Since the wheat is milled first, most of the grist at the bottom of the mash tun is wheat. Some wheat

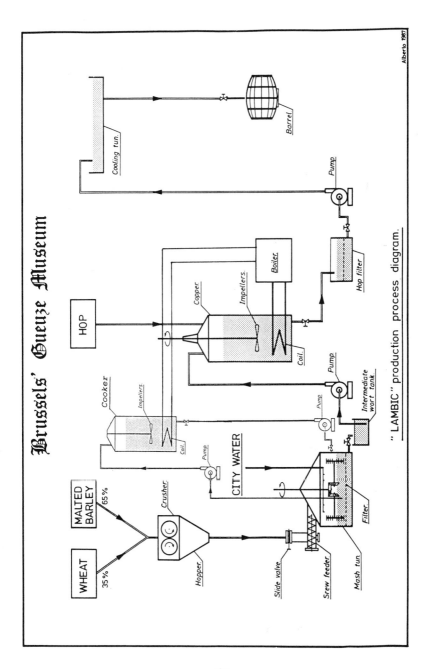

Brussels' Gueuze Museum

HOP

WHEAT 35% · MALTED BARLEY 65%

Hopper · Crusher · Slide valve · Srew feeder · Mash tun · Filter · CITY WATER · Pump · Intermediate wort tank · Pump · Cooker · Impellers · Coil · Copper · Impellers · Coil · Boiler · Hop filter · Pump · Cooling tun. · Barrel · Pump

Alberto 1987

" LAMBIC " production process diagram.

chaff might be mixed with the grist before mashing for the purpose of facilitating lautering. Alternatively, after the false-bottom of the mash tun has been covered with hot water, wheat chaff may be layered on top of the water before the grist is sent into the tun.

The mashing of lambic beers follows a temperature profile. The temperature changes are achieved by decoction (boiling) of portions of the mash, and by injecting boiling water to the main mash several times during the mashing process. The initial temperature of the mash is from 113 to 120 degrees F (45 to 48 degrees C). This is achieved with a strike water temperature of about 144 degrees F (62 degrees C). The water/grist ratio is very high, typically 8:1 or even 9:1 by weight at the end of mashing, when all the water has been added to the mash. Because the wheat starches are not modified, the mash has a milky-white appearance. A ten-minute rest is allowed after the steeping (*empatage*) of the grist is complete.

The temperature of the mash is brought up to 136 degrees F (58 degrees C) by injecting boiling water through the filter plates at the bottom of the mash vessel. About one-fifth (18 percent) of the total volume of the mash is pumped into a cooker (*macérateur*) and boiled gently. The temperature of the main mash is increased to 149 degrees F (65 degrees C) by injecting more boiling water through the bottom of the vessel. Another one-fifth (18 percent) of the main mash is pumped to the cooker where it is boiled. The contents of the cooker are then pumped back into the mash vessel. This brings the temperature of the mash up to 162 degrees F (72 degrees C). Conversion of the starch into sugars takes about twenty minutes. Even at these low temperatures, the amylase enzymes can be denatured before all the starch has been converted. A starch haze may remain visible even after mashing off at 170 degrees F (76 degrees C) with one last infusion with boiling water. The mash-mixing devices are turned off at this point and the mash is allowed to settle for twenty minutes.

Alternatively, some lambic brewers mix all the wheat flour with a small amount of malt and bring it to a boil in the cooker before returning it to the main mash. This process is identical to the American mashing process with adjunct (corn or rice).

The mashing process takes about two-and-a-half hours. The wort is then lautered through the bottom filter plates. The first worts are recirculated until clear. Sparging begins as soon as the grain bed is visible. The device used for sparging, a cross-shaped rotating head, is called a "Scottish cross" because it delivers water in scarce quantities. The temperature of the sparging water traditionally is about 173 degrees F (72 degrees C). However, the lambic brewer intends to obtain highly dextrinous wort. This is why the temperature of the sparging water might be raised even to 200 degrees F (95 degrees C) to solubilize any starch that might be left in the grist. The late worts usually stain iodine blue, indicating the presence of soluble and insoluble starch. Starch and dextrins are not undesirable in lambic wort. With time (remember that the fermentation takes about two years), most carbohydrates are eventually degraded and converted to various fermentation products by the mixed microbial flora of yeast and bacteria in the lambic fermentation.

A multiple-stage infusion method is another alternative used by some lambic brewers. Mash-in is at 95 degrees F (35 degrees C). By additions of boiling water, the mash temperature is brought up to 113 degrees F (45 degrees C), 131 degrees F (55 degrees C), and 149 degrees F (65 degrees C), each stage lasting about fifteen minutes. After mash-off at 162 to 164 degrees F (72 to 73 degrees C), the whole mash is pumped into the kettle where it is brought to a boil. It is then

Kettles for boiling the lambic wort. De Neve Brewery.

pumped back into the mash tun (which now acts as a lauter tun), where it sits for fifteen minutes. Once lautering is under way, sparging begins, with the water at 200 degrees F (95 degrees C). The amount of sparging water applied, or the duration of sparging, is a function of the desired final gravity.

· Wort Boiling ·

The wort is pumped into a copper kettle equipped with impellers and coils for a vigorous and uniform boil. The aged hops are added at the beginning of the boil. The hopping rate is about 2.5 pounds per 100 pounds of grain or from 21 and 27 ounces of hops per barrel of finished beer (500 to 650 g/hL). This value is much higher than what is common in the ale and lager brewing industry because the hops have lost most of their bittering power. The wort is boiled for at least three-and-a-half hours to as long as six hours. The extensive boil compensates for the high water/ grist ratio by evaporating a huge amount of water. Indeed, the volume of the wort is reduced by up to 30 percent during the boil. The hot wort is then pumped into the hop filter (*bac à houblon*) where the spent hops are recovered.

Until recently, faro was made by blending equal amounts of lambic and mars beer, and adding candy sugar to the blend. In that case, the first worts were used for lambic, and the late worts were used for mars beer. They had to be kept separate from that stage of the process until blending after fermentation. The high-gravity lambic wort was boiled in the kettle, and the low-gravity mars wort was boiled in the cooker-turned-kettle for a few hours.

- Wort Cooling, Aeration and Inoculation -

Cooling, aeration, and inoculation (using the local microbial flora) of the wort are conducted in an unusual fashion, which is unique to the brewing of lambic beers. From the hop filter, the wort is pumped into a cooling tun (*bac refroidissoir*), which is very wide and shallow (about forty square feet in area and one foot deep in most lambic breweries). Because the wort is spread over a large area, a considerable surface area is exposed to the atmosphere. This copper cooling tun is located in the highest part of the brewery — the loft up under the tile roof. Outdoor air is allowed to enter the loft between the vented tiles and through open louvers. It is so important to leave the local microbial flora undisturbed that a Brussels' brewer, whose roof was in precarious shape, elected to cover the old tiles with new tiles rather than to rebuild his roof from scratch, convinced as he was that the tiles housed a host of precious microorganisms. The more modern breweries, however, are equipped with a complex system of fans that evenly distributes the flow of air over the wort. The wort is left overnight to settle, cool, and pick up the oxygen and the microbial flora that are required for the lambic fermentation.

The next morning (between 5 and 9 a.m. depending on the weather), the wort has cooled down to 68 to 73 degrees F (20 to 23 degrees C) and is ready to be racked into the wooden casks where the fermentation starts after a few days. First, it is pumped from the cooling tun into a mixing tun (*cuve guilloire*) to obtain a homogeneous liquid. From there, it is pumped into individual casks.

For the production of faro, the lambic and mars worts — which, remember, have been processed separately — are cooled and inoculated in the cooling tun and mixing tun, respectively.

THE OLD BREWING PROCESS

It is interesting to see how the brewing process for lambic beers has evolved over the years. Compared to the main brewing industry, the lambic industry is a very traditional one. And yet very significant changes have occurred. In consulting European brewing manuals from the 1850s, I was able to reconstruct the lambic brewing process as it was in those days.

Equal amounts of unmalted wheat and malted barley were used to produce the traditional lambic, faro, and mars beer. The malt was barley, germinated slowly and very lightly kilned. The grains were mixed together and coarse-milled. First, water at 113 degrees F (45 degrees C) was poured into the mash tun to cover the false bottom by a few inches. Then, two or three "bags" of wheat chaff were layered on the bottom, followed by the grist and the water until the tun was full. The mash liquor consisted of water at 113 degrees F (45 degrees C) injected through the false bottom and

Hot lambic wort poured into the cooling tun (*bac refroidissoir*). Cantillon Brewery.

boiling striking water poured onto the grist and quickly mixed in by mechanical devices. About 220 pounds (100 kg) of grist yielded 2.2 barrels (260 L) each of lambic and mars beer, or 3.9 barrels (460 L) of faro.

The surface of the mash was covered with a small layer of wheat chaff. Conical wicker-baskets (*stuyk manden*), as deep as the mashing vessel and about three feet in diameter, were immediately placed on top of the mash and pushed deep into it to separate the liquor from the grist. The turbid mashing liquor collected inside the baskets would then be scooped with copper pans (*kleyn ketels*) and dumped into a kettle (*slym-ketel*), where it was heated to a boil with the clear liquid simultaneously run off the false bottom of the mash tun. Boiling water was added to the grist in the mash tun, and a second mashing stage was conducted. The liquid portion of the mash was separated from the spent grain as before, and boiled in the kettle with the first portion for twenty minutes. In the meantime, the spent grains were pushed to the sides of the mash tun, the false bottom was covered with a new layer of wheat chaff, the bed of spent grains was reconstructed on top of it, and the boiled liquid (*slym*) was returned to the mash tun. The mash was mixed again carefully without disturbing the bottom layer. It was allowed to settle for one hour, and the wort was then run off through the false bottom. Two additional mashing stages were conducted with boiling water in the same fashion, thereby achieving the equivalent of sparging operations in modern brewing. As mentioned previously, the late worts run off after these two mashing stages had a lower gravity than the first worts and were used to make faro and mars beer, whereas lambic was produced only from the first worts.

The wort for lambic production was boiled in the kettle for five to six hours with 32 to 36 ounces of Alost or Poperinhge hops per barrel of wort (780 to 860 g/hL). Then the boiled wort was poured into the hop strainer, cooled, and oxygenated in a wort cooler, a large, vertical copper plate open to the atmosphere, on each side of which the wort trickled as a thin film. It was collected at 50 to 60 degrees F (10 to 15 degrees C), depending on the weather, in the mixing tun. The wort was immediately distributed into casks without any artificial inoculation.

The same process was applied to the late worts for mars beer except that these were boiled in the cooker. The stage in which the wort picked up the microbial flora from the brewery atmosphere did not exist at the time. Some brewers, however, added to the cool wort in the mixing tun about 5 percent wort that had not been boiled. This wort had been sitting in the open for a few hours and had picked up microbes from the surroundings. These microorganisms caused the fermentation to start faster. The wort for faro and mars beer production was boiled for twelve to fifteen hours with the spent hops from the lambic boil, and 17 to 21 ounces of hops per barrel of wort (400 to 500 g/hL), before it was processed as described for lambic wort.

The filled casks were then transported within the next twenty-four hours to the fermentation cellar where they were stored in up to three levels with their bung-hole left open. The casks were regularly refilled during the spring and summer of the first year to compensate for fermentation and evaporation losses so the beer would not oxidize. Fermentation would start after a few days or a few months and last for eight to twenty months. Lambic beer was not considered ready before two years. The gravity of the lambic wort ranged from 1.050 to 1.060 (12 to 15 degrees Plato) to 1.015 to 1.020 (3.8 to 6 degrees Plato) over these two years.

Why did brewers then not intend for the wort to pick up as much natural microbial flora as possible, as is presently the case with the use of the cooling tun? In the 1850s, the presence of a lactic flavor or a ropy appearance (caused by lactic acid bacteria and considered "normal" in today's lambic fermentations) was regarded as a defect. It was felt that by shortening the exposure of the wort to the environment, such contamination was avoided. It is likely that the agents of the lambic fermentation came mostly from the casks in which the wort was placed.

5

Lambic Fermentation and Cellaring

MICROBIOLOGY OF THE LAMBIC FERMENTATION

The microbiology of lambic beers is what makes them so unique. Lambic beers undergo a "spontaneous" or "natural" fermentation, that is, they are fermented by the microbial flora found in the brewery and the atmosphere surrounding it. This practice in itself is not so unique and many great wines are still made this way today in such famous wine-making regions as Bordeaux or Burgundy. It is the *resulting combination of microorganisms* involved in the lambic fermentation that is unique. It is comprised of both yeasts and bacteria, a truly surprising fact for most brewers who recognize yeast — but not just any yeast, only *Saccharomyces cerevisiae* or *Saccharomyces carlsbergensis* — as the only agents that may turn their wort into a quality beer, and rightfully fear bacteria as the agents of beer contamination or spoilage.

Indeed, if we look at the history of brewing, top-fermenting *S. cerevisiae* for the making of ales, and bottom-fermenting *S. carlsbergensis* for the making of lagers, are the only desirable yeast species in a brewery. Other yeasts,

71

which may belong to the genera *Saccharomyces, Brettanomyces, Dekkera, Kloeckera, Hansenula, Candida, Pichia, Hanseniaspora, Cryptococcus,* and *Rhodotorula,* are regarded as contaminants and are usually grouped under the term "wild yeast," as in "out of the brewer's control." Similarly, the few bacterial genera that can tolerate the drastic conditions of pH, alcohol, and hop resins in beer — as well as the yeast used to ferment it — are dreaded contaminants. They include lactic acid bacteria (*Pediococcus* and *Lactobacillus*), acetic acid bacteria (*Acetobacter* and *Acetomonas*), enteric bacteria (*Klebsiella* and *Hafnia*), and *Zymomonas.* These bacteria spoil the flavor of beer. However, they do not endanger the health of the consumer, that is, they are not pathogenic. Fortunately, pathogenic microorganisms fail to grow or survive in beer for extended periods because of beer's low pH and high alcohol content.

Although we sometimes speak of fermentation as "controlled spoilage," because we now understand this vital microbial process and have developed the modern technologies to control it, lambic fermentations remain an exception in that we often lose control of them. One of the purposes of this text, however, is to offer a way of producing lambiclike beers through a "controlled" fermentation process. If we quickly review the list of the main organisms involved in lambic fermentation (*Saccharomyces, Brettanomyces, Dekkera, Kloeckera, Pediococcus,* and enteric bacteria), we find that all but the first one are usually associated with beer spoilage. As brewers, we should therefore refer to the lambic fermentation as a combination and sequence of "desirable" spoilages, if not entirely "controlled" ones. As lambic drinkers, on the other hand, we should avoid using the word "spoilage" out of respect for the skilled (and susceptible) brewers who produce it.

As mentioned previously, traditional lambic fermentations take about two years. Based on the very thorough studies of Professor Verachtert and his collaborators at the University of Leuven in Belgium, we know that several microorganisms work in sequence to produce the unique flavor of lambic beers. The following pattern of microbial development is observed. Three to seven days after the wort has been cooled and allowed to pick up microorganisms from the atmosphere, fermentation starts with the development of wort enteric bacteria and strains of *Kloeckera apiculata*. After three to four weeks, these organisms are overgrown by strains of *S. cerevisiae* and *S. bayanus,* and these are responsible for the main, alcoholic fermentation, which lasts for three to four months. A strong bacterial activity is observed next. Strains of *Pediococcus damnosus,* a lactic acid bacterium, take over the fermentation. These organisms reach their maximum density during the summer months and cause a five-fold increase in lactic acid concentration and a big drop in pH. They may also cause ropiness in some casks. At this stage, the presence of air in the casks may favor the development of acetic acid bacteria of the genus *Acetobacter* and cause spoilage of the beer.

After eight months, a new population of yeast cells is found in the beers. These are strains of *Brettanomyces bruxellensis* and *Brettanomyces lambicus.* They are responsible for a further reduction of the residual extract and the development of special flavors. Oxidative yeasts of the genera *Candida, Pichia, Hansenula,* and *Cryptococcus* may also be detected after the main fermentation and may cause the formation of a film on the beer surface.

In all, as many as a dozen kinds of microorganisms may participate in the fermentation of a lambic beer! The reader should now begin to realize the complexity of such a beer. It requires a great deal more microorganisms than ales or lagers, and these organisms have to work in a particular sequence. The possibility of spoilage also exists! What a challenge for a brewer! This gives rise to the need for a discussion of the organisms in the sequence in which they appear during the lambic fermentation, their main features and characteristics and their contribution to the character of lambic beers. (The pattern of microbial development during the lambic fermentation is summarized in Figure 3.)

- Enteric bacteria -
(3 to 7 days)

Enteric bacteria in the wort reach a very high cell concentration within a few days after cooling of the wort. Concentrations of 10^8 cells/mL after two weeks are common. The viability of these enteric bacteria decreases rapidly, and after two months they are usually absent from the fermenting wort. Enteric bacteria or *Enterobacteriaceae* are gram-negative bacteria. Some of the strains found in lambic fermentations are closely related to the most well-known example of the family, *Escherichia coli*, strains of which are present in large numbers in the gut of mammals. They may include species of *Citrobacter, Enterobacter, Klebsiella,* and *Hafnia.*

In wort, they produce a variety of flavors and aromas ranging from sweet, honey, and fruity to vegetable and fecal. Enteric bacteria can readily utilize glucose in wort for their growth. However, they cannot use maltose or maltotriose, the main sugars in wort. They metabolize glucose into lactic acid, acetic acid, ethanol and carbon dioxide through the so-called "mixed-acid fermentation." Most of the acetic acid found in the final product is synthesized at this early stage of the fermentation, mostly by these enteric bacteria. The mixed-acid fermentation (which results

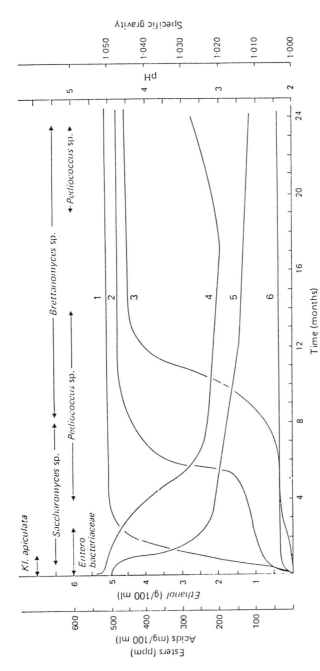

Figure 3. Evolution of some important parameters of spontaneous lambic fermentation: 1 = ethanol; 2 = lactic acid; 3 = ethyl lactate; 4 = pH; 5 = real extract; 6 = acetic acid, and sequence of microorganisms involved (Reprinted from Van Oevelen *et al.* 1977. *J. Inst. Brew.* 83:356-360).

in the emission of CO_2) is responsible for the formation of foam at this stage. The enteric bacteria consume most of the aminoacids available in the lambic wort and produce a variety of amines and peptides that impart a very peculiar (and temporary) flavor to the lambic. The aminoacid depletion is believed to account for the very slow start of the main, alcoholic fermentation (Verachtert; 1983).

Since wort *Enterobacteriaceae* are known to produce several sulfur compounds, carbonyls, and phenols, they definitely contribute to the flavor of lambic beers, although some of these early fermentation products disappear during later phases, entrapped by the CO_2 bubbles from the main fermentation. Dimethyl sulfide (DMS) is a good illustration of this phenomenon. Significant amounts of DMS — up to 450 parts per billion (ppb) — are produced by enteric bacteria during the first two weeks of the fermentation (Van Oevelen *et al.*; 1978). The DMS concentration falls to 100 ppb after most of it has been stripped by fermentation gases.

- Kloeckera apiculata -
(3 to 7 days)

Strains of the yeast *Kloeckera apiculata* are found in the wort at the same time as the enteric bacteria, that is, during the first two weeks of fermentation. Maximum concentrations of 10^5 cells/mL are found after a week. After two weeks, *Kloeckera* is overgrown by *Saccharomyces* species and disappears. The same phenomenon is observed in the spontaneous fermentations of wine and cider. This similarity could account for some of the winey and cidery characters of lambic beers. *Kloeckera* ferments glucose but not maltose. The fermentation is a mixed-acid fermentation, similar but not identical to the one observed with enteric bacteria. The very fast growth of *K. apiculata* and of wort

Enterobacteriaceae results in a decrease in pH from 5.1 to 4.6, as a result of the synthesis of acetic and lactic acids.

One interesting property of the yeast *K. apiculata* is the ability to secrete proteases (enzymes that break down proteins) into the medium in which they are growing. Although the yeast does not survive for a long time in the wort (two weeks at most) and does not reach a very high cell density (10^5 cells/mL of wort), we believe that it contributes to breaking down a significant amount of the wort proteins that did not precipitate during the boil. That amount is higher than in all-malt wort because of the wheat used in the mash. Indeed, wheat is a cereal with a particularly high protein content. Proteins are partially responsible for chill haze in beer, and it is therefore beneficial to have a yeast with some proteolytic activity at some point in the fermentation. The contribution of *K. apiculata* to the flavor of the final product is minor, namely a few esters with floral and fruity characters, which are probably stripped off during the main fermentation because of their high volatility.

- Saccharomyces species -
(2 weeks)

After two weeks, *K. apiculata* is overgrown by yeast strains belonging to the *Saccharomyces* genus. These strains perform the main alcoholic fermentation and are responsible for most of the attenuation of the wort. They dominate the wort's microbial flora during the first seven months of fermentation, reaching maximum cell densities of about 5×10^6 cells/mL after three to four weeks. Such a cell density is still well below the densities of 10^8 cells/mL found in commercial top or bottom fermentations.

The isolates found in the lambic wort belong to either of two species, *S. bayanus* or *S. cerevisiae*. *S. bayanus* is now

77

considered as a race of the species *S. cerevisiae* according to the latest yeast classification by Kreger-van Rij (1984). Both races are very vigorous fermenters of glucose, maltose, and in some cases maltotriose, the main sugars in wort. Another race of the species *S. cerevisiae, S. globosus,* is found less regularly during the fermentation and at a much lower density (no more than 10^3 cells/mL). It does not ferment maltose, a limitation which likely accounts for its minor role in the lambic fermentation. Despite the fact that *Saccharomyces* species ferment most of the sugar in lambic wort, they are not the main contributors to the characteristic flavor of lambic beers.

- **Lactic acid bacteria** -
(3 to 4 months)

After three to four months, the main fermentation is complete. The yeast population decreases, while the bacterial population increases. Most bacterial isolates found during that period are lactic acid bacteria of the genera *Pediococcus,* of which the predominant species usually is *P. damnosus.* Some *Lactobacillus* isolates may also be found. The population of lactic acid bacteria reaches a maximum after seven months, which coincides with the beginning of summer. The warmer temperature in the cellar around that time of the year seems to be required for lactic acid bacteria to grow. Indeed, the same phenomenon is observed during the second year of the lambic fermentation; that is, the population of lactic acid bacteria peaks again at the onset of the second summer. We suspect that one way to speed up the lambic fermentation would be to set the casks at a warmer temperature as soon as the main, alcoholic fermentation is complete. This could simply be achieved by having temperature-controlled cellars, a luxury that few lambic breweries can afford because of their old age (the buildings usually are not very well insulated).

Tolerance to hop antiseptic is important in *P. damnosus*, which grows in hopped wort while other species of lactic acid bacteria are inhibited. As lactic acid bacteria, *P. damnosus* ferment glucose into lactic acid without emitting carbon dioxide. Their presence in the lambic fermentation coincides with the large increase in lactic acid concentration observed after a few months. Lactic acid is responsible for the sour taste of lambic beers. It is definitely one of the key components of lambic flavor. The increase in lactic acid concentration during bacterial proliferation is rather slow, however, because these bacteria are very fastidious (slow-growing, with complex nutritional requirements) and never reach a very high cell density in the lambic wort. *P. damnosus* strains readily produce acetoin and diacetyl which may contribute a buttery aroma to the beer. Diacetyl concentrations of greater than 200 ppb are produced by *Pediococcus*. However, these levels later drop to about 45 ppb (Van Oevelen *et al.*; 1978).

Frequently, a disorder develops at this stage of the lambic fermentation that makes the beer oily or even ropy. The ropiness may be accompanied or followed by a haze that cannot be eliminated by filtration. In 1900, Van Laer published the first account of a rope-forming bacterium in lambic worts. The bacterium, which was called *Bacillus viscosus bruxellensis* at the time, was thought to be responsible for the appearance of ropiness in some casks. This disorder is caused by some strains of *P. damnosus* (formerly *P. cerevisiae*), which may produce slime from glucose or maltose in the wort (Van Oevelen and Verachtert; 1979). The slime is composed of carbohydrates, nucleic acids, and proteins. Its effect is only aesthetic, and it is not harmful to the consumer. Fortunately, if slime is produced, it is usually hydrolyzed later during the lambic fermentation by grow-ing cells of *Brettanomyces* yeasts.

It is also worth mentioning the occasional presence of some acetic acid bacteria after the main fermentation pe-riod, but at irregular times and in variable amounts. We suspect that poor handling of the casks resulting in the lambic wort being exposed to air causes contamination by acetic acid bacteria in addition to damage to the beer by oxidation. Indeed, acetic acid bacteria are strict aerobes, that is, they cannot grow without oxygen. In other words, their presence in the lambic fermentation is not regarded as a desirable feature and can be avoided by keeping the casks full.

- Yeasts of the Brettanomyces genus -
(8 months)

After about eight months of fermentation, the yeast population increases again. This time, it is dominated by strains belonging to the species *Brettanomyces bruxellensis* and *Brettanomyces lambicus*. These strains remain in the lambic wort for the next sixteen months and are the main contributors to the aroma of lambic beers. Their growth coincides with a further slow decrease in residual extract. Organisms of the genus *Brettanomyces* have at various times been part of the history of brewing. The earliest reference to *Brettanomyces* is a patent for the use of these organisms in the secondary fermentation of English beers, which was taken out in 1903 by N. Hjelte Claussen, a brewing micro-biologist in Copenhagen at Carlsberg Brewery. Unfortu-nately for Claussen's discovery, the strength of British beers, owing to an increase in the taxation of their alcohol content, began to decline. British brewers, instead of welcoming Claussen's outstanding work as it deserved, decided that the type of flavor produced by *Brettanomyces* was no longer desirable. Who says brewers are not practical people?

Brettanomyces species are still fairly common organisms in top-fermentation breweries, but they now belong in the ranks of ignominious contaminants. These organisms are very difficult to get rid of in a brewery, especially one that is fairly old. They are found in the atmosphere of the brewery and inside the wood fibers of the casks used in the lambic fermentation. An interesting situation exists in the French wine industry. Some wines of great reputation are infected with *Brettanomyces,* which is then said to add to the complexity and delicacy of the flavor. Tullo, at the Guinness brewery, had already isolated in 1899 two types of "secondary yeast" from Irish stout. This exported beer depended indeed on these yeasts not only for its characteristic flavor, but also for the production of CO_2 in the bottle due to their apparent ability to ferment higher polysaccharides (those we today call dextrins), which the "primary yeast" (*Saccharomyces*) could not ferment. In 1940, Custers published an outstanding monograph on *Brettanomyces,* which reported the first systematic investigation of the genus. In all, he studied seventeen different strains isolated from English ale and stout, and from lambic beer.

At this point, it is necessary to review the regulation of sugar metabolism in yeast (as investigated mostly in the genus *Saccharomyces*) in order to understand what makes *Brettanomyces* such a unique organism. Carbohydrate metabolism is carefully regulated in yeast. Since glucose utilization yields more energy by aerobic respiration than by alcoholic fermentation, yeasts respire whenever they can, especially in the presence of high oxygen and low sugar concentration, and thereby increase biomass or cell density. This phenomenon is known as the "Pasteur effect." It is exemplified by the commercial production of bakers' yeast from molasses when the "fermentation" (it actually is a respiration) is carried out in highly aerated vessels, and the molasses is pulsed into the vessels in small increments that maintain the concentration of fermentable sugar at or below 0.5 percent. On the other hand, glucose concentrations in excess of 0.5 percent or so, even in the presence of oxygen, are fermented by yeast into ethanol and CO_2; this phenomenon is known as the "Crabtree effect."

One of the most interesting characteristics of the metabolism of *Brettanomyces* is that young aerobic cultures exhibit a negative Pasteur effect, that is, they have a very much stronger fermentative ability under aerobic conditions than under anaerobic conditions, unlike all other yeasts. This property is consistent with their ability to form a film or pellicle on the surface of the beer inside the casks. All lambic brewers make it very clear that this pellicle (which is probably made of yeasts of the genera *Pichia* and *Candida* in addition to *Brettanomyces*) is not to be cracked at any time during the fermentation or the beer will be damaged by oxidation.

Another important characteristic of the genus *Brettanomyces* is that secondary products of fermentation accumulate to a much greater extent than is the case with *Saccharomyces*. These secondary products are crucially important to the lambic character. Although they still account for only a small proportion of the total fermented sugars, they comprise many different kinds of compounds, each in a fairly low concentration, but many with even lower detection thresholds (easily smelled or tasted at low concentration). Chief among these compounds are the esters ethyl acetate and ethyl lactate. These esters may be formed chemically or enzymatically (by the enzyme called *esterase*) as a result of the reaction between an organic acid and an alcohol. Unlike *Kloeckera* and *Saccharomyces, Brettanomyces* yeasts display a high esterase activity (Spaepen and Verachtert; 1982). The esterase enzyme can work both ways; that is, it can trigger either the synthesis of an ester from an organic acid and an alcohol, or the hydrolysis of the ester into the acid and the alcohol.

The unique contribution of *Brettanomyces* to the lambic flavor is the result of a high synthesis by its esterase of ethyl acetate and ethyl lactate from ethanol and acetic and lactic acids, and to the hydrolysis by that same esterase of the iso-amyl acetate produced earlier in the fermentation by *Saccharomyces*. Some acetic acid is sometimes produced by *Brettanomyces* yeasts at this stage of the fermentation. *Brettanomyces* strains may also develop a strong horsey flavor, which is very objectionable at high concentration. This phenomenon is especially acute in wines infected with the organism. In lambic beers, however, the horsey character may be strong or weak, depending on the conditions of the fermentation. What causes this character to appear is not yet well understood. The compounds responsible for it are tetrahydropyridines (Heresztyn; 1986 a, b). It seems that they might only be produced when ethanol and the amino-acid lysine are present in the growth medium. Since wort contains lysine and ethanol once the fermentation is under way, the conditions are set for the horsey flavor to be produced when *Brettanomyces* is the predominant species in lambic wort. At a low level, nevertheless, it is a desirable part of the lambic flavor.

The contribution of the *Brettanomyces* species to lambic flavor, although paramount, is very slow, as was the case with the *Pediococcus* species. The reason is identical. *Brettanomyces* species are fastidious (slow) growers, and their cell density in lambic wort remains relatively low even at the late stages of the fermentation. The constituency of the microbial flora differs between Brussels and its surroundings.

Whereas *B. bruxellensis* is the predominant yeast in the city, *B. lambicus* is the main yeast in the country-side breweries. Their respective contributions to the flavor of lambic beers is different. René Lindemans' comment that "the wild yeast (*Brettanomyces*) is better in the country that in Brussels — which is contaminated by city smog" likely relates to the above-mentioned difference in the make up of the flora.

- Yeasts of the genera Pichia, Candida, Hansenula and Cryptococcus -
(8 months)

Oxidative yeasts of the genera *Pichia, Candida, Hansenula,* and *Cryptococcus* also are detected late in lambic fermentations and are responsible (along with *Brettanomyces*) for the formation of a film on the surface of the beer after the main fermentation. It is believed that they produce a few esters and other volatiles that may contribute slightly to the fruity/cidery character of lambic beers. *Hansenula* and *Pichia* produce large quantities of ethyl acetate by aerobic fermentation. The predominant species are *Candida lambica* and its perfect counterpart *Pichia fermentans*. These yeasts are found at the surface of the beer because they are oxidative and because they form a pseudomycelium (semi-solid network of branched chains of elongated cells), which gives them the ability to float.

- A Specific Sequence -

The conclusion of the extensive studies of Professor Verachtert and his collaborators at the University of Leuven, Belgium, and of our own experiments at the University of California at Davis on the microbiology of the lambic fermentation, is that the main microbial species involved in the lambic fermentation are (in this sequence):

- wort *Enterobacteriaceae* (bacteria),
- *Kloeckera apiculata* (yeast),
- *Saccharomyces* species (yeast),
- *Pediococcus damnosus* (bacteria), and
- *Brettanomyces* species (yeast).

Because it is a spontaneous fermentation, the lambic fermentation is very hard to control, and the resulting lambic may vary considerably. Indeed, casks filled with wort from the same brew, cooled, and inoculated in the same conditions, can produce very different lambics. This indicates that potential microbial infections from the wooden fibers in the casks, handling of the casks by the brewer, and oxygen level in the casks are key factors in the lambic fermentation. Casks lying in dry places or near vibrating machinery risk spoilage by acetic acid bacteria because oxygen can get into the lambic through the wood and/or through the broken film of surface yeast. Some extreme types of lambics obtained as a result of uncontrolled conditions include hard lambic characterized by a sharp, sour taste and fruity aroma associated with very high acetic acid and ethyl acetate levels from spoilage by acetic acid bacteria; soft lambic characterized by a low acidity, an astringent mouthfeel, and a celerylike flavor from insufficient bacterial seeding and growth; and ropy lambic characterized by an oily texture resulting from high amounts of pediococci.

PRODUCTS OF THE LAMBIC FERMENTATION

Various products comprise the unique flavor of lambic and gueuze beers, and they are produced in a sequence that follows very closely the sequence of microorganisms. Van Oevelen *et al.* (1976), Spaepen *et al.* (1978), and Van Oevelen *et al.* (1978) studied the evolution of some key lambic components over a twenty four-month fermentation period. (Their findings are reproduced in Figure 4.)

- Phase One of Fermentation -

The first phase of the fermentation takes about three months during which most of the ethanol is produced and about 80 percent of the sugars are consumed, mostly by *Saccharomyces* yeast. The synthesis of higher alcohols (propanol, amyl alcohol, isobutanol, isoamyl alcohol, and phenethyl alcohol) closely follows the synthesis of ethanol.

Acetic acid is produced in large amounts during the first month by Enteric bacteria. In some casks infected with acetic acid bacteria (which would indicate poor protection of the beer against oxygen since these bacteria are strict aerobes), the level of acetic acid can reach 4,000 mg/L. An important amount of the main ester ethyl acetate is produced during the first phase of fermentation in part because its precursors — ethanol and acetic acid — are already present. The concentration of ethyl acetate continues to increase through the second phase of the fermentation.

Two fatty acids — caprylic (C_8) and capric (C_{10}) acids — and the corresponding esters ethyl caprylate and ethyl caprate, are produced in the first phase of the fermentation by *Kloeckera* and *Saccharomyces* yeast. These contribute a very characteristic goaty, cheesy flavor to some lambic products. Fatty acids from C_{12} to C_{18} increase slowly during the first months. Myristic acid (C_{14}) and the higher unsaturated fatty acids $C_{18:2}$ (linoleic), and $C_{18:3}$ (linolenic) are produced early on by enterobacteria.

- Phase Two of Fermentation -

The second phase of the fermentation starts with the lowering of the pH by *Pediococcus* bacteria. It lasts for up to two years during which the pH might drop from 4 to 3. This

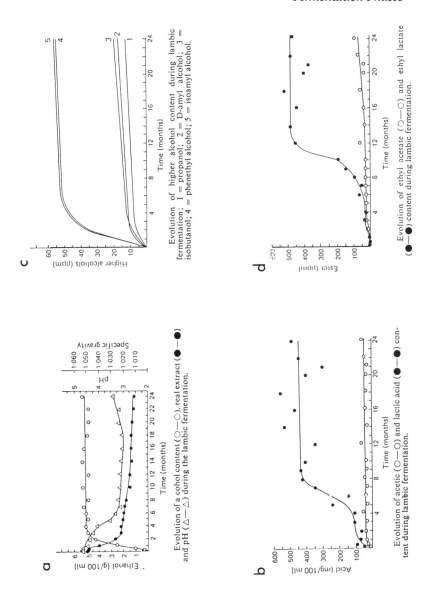

Figure 4. Evolution of some important parameters of spontaneous lambic fermentation: (a) ethanol, real extract and pH; (b) acetic and lactic acids; (c) higher alcohols; and (d) ethyl acetate and ethyl lactate (Reprinted from Van Oevelen *et al.* 1976. *J. Inst. Brew.* 82:322-326).

drop is due mostly to the conversion of sugars into lactic acid by pediococci. The residual extract is lowered further from 1.022 to 1.012, half of that reduction taking place in the first six to eight months. The concentration of ethanol remains constant because little is produced by *Brettanomyces* yeast, barely enough to compensate for losses due to evaporation or esterification.

About 800 mg/L of lactic acid is found after the first month of fermentation. There is a slight increase in lactic acid during the next five to six months followed by a large, two- to five-fold increase as the second phase of the fermentation takes place. Exceptionally high values of up to 13 g/L may be found in ropy lambics. A large increase in ethyl lactate follows the increase in lactic acid concentration. Maximum levels of ethyl lactate are usually obtained about three months after lactic acid has reached its highest concentration. Interestingly, the high levels of the esters ethyl acetate and ethyl lactate cannot be explained by chemical esterification only (the simple reaction between an alcohol and an acid), indicating that some enzymatic synthesis is effected by the microorganisms involved.

The concentration of isoamyl acetate, an important ester in most beers, remains below the detection threshold of 0.5 mg/L. It is believed that what little isoamyl acetate is produced during the first phase of the fermentation by *Saccharomyces* is metabolized during the second phase by *Brettanomyces*. Higher fatty acids, such as caprylic and capric acids are known growth-promoting factors for many yeasts. Among other things, they make these yeasts ethanol-tolerant. It is possible that the high amounts of these fatty acids produced during the first months of the lambic fermentation promote the growth of the unusual yeast flora found in lambic during the second phase of the fermentation when the ethanol concentration is already high.

The concentrations of caprylic (C_8) and capric (C_{10}) acids increase slowly but steadily during the later months of the fermentation, along with the concentration of lauric acid (C_{12}). This production pattern is ascribed to *Brettanomyces* yeast. The resulting flavor is a key part of the *Brettanomyces* character in lambic. The level of the higher unsaturated fatty acids decreases as the lambic becomes older and some disappear completely, especially $C_{18:2}$ (linoleic) and $C_{18:3}$ (linolenic) because they are taken up by yeasts and pediococci.

Up to 200 ppb of DMS are formed by wort *Enterobacteriaceae* during the first two weeks of the fermentation. DMS levels fall below 100 ppb after the main fermentation as a result of stripping by fermentation gases. Diacetyl concentrations of more than 200 ppb are produced by *Pediococcus* strains after the main fermentation. These levels decrease to about 45 ppb during the later phase of the lambic fermentation.

FERMENTATION EQUIPMENT AND PROCEDURES

- Fermentation Casks -

Brussels used to harbor the commerce of the finest European wines. Wine merchants, after selling their Spanish, Portuguese, and French wines in Northern Europe, would sell the wooden casks in which the wines were transported to British and Belgian brewers. Today, the lambic fermentation is still carried out in these used casks from the Cognac, Porto, Sherry, and Madeira regions — and even from Bordeaux although these are used to a lesser extent because of their prohibitive price. Fermentation casks are classified according to their capacity. The *tonne* or *tonneau bruxellois* is 2.2 barrels (267 L), the *pipe* has a capacity of 5.5 barrels (650 L), and the *foudre* holds 25 barrels (3000 L). Made

89

of oak or chestnut wood, these wine barrels have a round bung hole, unlike beer barrels. Once they are in a brewery, however, a rectangular bung-hole four by six inches is cut to allow for cleaning, and the barrels are sulfur-fumigated to control mold growth.

The lambic brewer must be an accomplished cooper's craftsman to keep his casks in good condition. An alternative chosen by the Belle-Vue brewery is to employ a number of coopers or apprentices. The barrels must be carefully cleaned before filling. This is a very delicate task because of the need for preserving certain microorganisms required for the fermentation of lambics and to protect the beer against unwanted infections.

The casks are rolled to a part of the brewery devoted only to barrel cleaning operations. They are first cleaned manually with a special brush (*ramon*), the bristles of which are of birchwood sticks. This brush removes most of the lees (*dik-dik*) or sediments and solids left after drawing off the

Cooperage shop (*atelier de tonnellerie*). Belle-Vue Brewery.

beer from the cask. Traditionally, the *dik-dik* was scrubbed out of the barrel and saved in a bucket. It turned sour and acetic after a few days, and the slurry was used to clean the brewery's copper vessels. Next, the barrel is cleaned with brushes, chains with sharp scraping edges and a hot water stream is applied inside the rotating barrel, leaving it clean and ready for use. Most brewers today add a steam injection to the cycle, although they make sure not to completely sterilize their casks before filling them with wort. The largest lambic brewery uses only a high-pressure, hot-water system to clean its casks. If the casks are not used immediately, they are sanitized with a burning sulfur tablet and plugged. Since these barrels are hard to find, the brewery repairs them rather than discard them when they begin to rot. It is not uncommon when walking through the fermentation cellars of a lambic brewery to run across old barrels with a few new staves.

If wooden casks are unavailable, oak chips in stainless steel fermentation and conditioning tanks are a cheap but efficient substitute. Their use is becoming widespread in large lambic breweries.

- Fermentation Cellars -

The fermentation cellars of a lambic brewery look just like winery cellars, with wooden casks stacked two or more levels high. The aisles need to be at least one barrel wide so the brewer has room to replace leaking ones. The most common method of cask storage is to place the larger *pipes* on pallets or cradles on the lower level and the smaller *tonnes* on top. The casks are stabilized by small wooden blocks called *slotjes*. Each cask bears the date the brew went into it. Each brewing year is identified with a letter of the alphabet. The visitor thus realizes that casks from up to four different years may be found in the cellars.

Spider webs are a common sight in the cellars of lambic breweries. Some brewers believe that the presence of spiders is essential to maintaining the proper microbial flora inside the brewery. The fermenting wort foaming out of open casks attracts lots of insects — especially fruit flies — which carry many undesirable microorganisms including wild yeast that might contaminate or spoil the wort. As predators of flies, the spiders *Tegenaria parietina, Lepthyphantes leprosus, Pholcus phalangioides,* and other varieties guard the lambic wort against such infections and are treated with respect and care by most lambic brewers. *Killing a spider in their brewery is considered a crime.*

- Fermentation Operations -

The fermentation casks are filled as soon as the wort has cooled down to about 64 degrees F (18 degrees C). The bung-hole is left open during the course of the main fermentation, letting out a white foam that turns brownish-yellow and hardens a few days into the fermentation, thereby forming a natural plug that limits the risks of oxidation and infection. The bung is closed after a few weeks to minimize oxidation of the beer. An additional protection against oxidation occurs when a film forms on the beer's surface as a result of oxidative yeasts of the *Brettanomyces, Pichia,* and *Candida* genera. A special effort is made to avoid vibrations and disturbances that might break this film. The temperature in the cellars naturally remains relatively constant because of limited fluctuations in the weather. Some very cold years, however, may bring freezing conditions into the cellars and cause some casks to explode if they are too full.

Foam gushing out of fermenting lambic casks. Cantillon Brewery.

Wooden casks serve a special role in the maturation of lambic by allowing a little oxygen to slowly contact the beer. This access, if sufficiently slow and limited, produces some of the desirable changes of aging and allows the microbial flora to develop better. Water and ethanol vapor also steadily escape from the cask. Depending on the relative humidity in the cellar, the aging lambic may become more (during dry conditions) or less (during moist conditions) concentrated in alcohol because of the different diffusion rates of ethanol and water through the wood. As water and alcohol escape, the real extract of the lambic increases slightly and the decrease in volume appears as ullage (headspace). This allows more air to enter the cask. To prevent oxidation, the ullage is lessened frequently by adding more of the same lambic from another cask, making sure not to disturb the film of yeast on top of the beer.

The science of lambic brewing is not an exact one, and many brews are lost to contamination because of barrel-to-barrel quality variations and poor temperature control. It is remarkable to observe how a batch of wort can yield completely different lambics after the fermentation and aging process have been completed. For some unexplained reason, the flora in a few barrels of every batch fails to complete the fermentation, and the lambic becomes contaminated with acetic acid bacteria and turns to vinegar. This lambic vinegar is sometimes used as a cleanser for the copper vessels and cooling tun.

LAMBIC, MARS AND FARO

Almost all the lambic brewed goes towards the production of gueuze and fruit lambics, although a small percentage is still sold as straight lambic, *lambic doux*, *vieux lambic*, and faro. Lambic in its basic form is hard to find, but it is sometimes served on draft in some cafés in Brussels and in the Senne Valley. If a brew of less than six months is sold, it is customarily identified as "young" (*jong*) or "fox" (*vos*) lambic. *Lambic doux* (sweet lambic) is lambic sweetened with sugar. It is the specialty of a few cafés, especially La Bécasse in Brussels.

The Cantillon brewery makes about 2,000 bottles of *vieux lambic* (aged lambic) every year. This limited production is not sold but is reserved for the distinguished visitors of the Gueuze Museum located at the Cantillon brewery. *Vieux lambic* is aged for three years in wood and one year in the bottle. It has a pinkish, sherrylike color and virtually no carbon dioxide. A 95 percent attenuation is not uncommon for this aged lambic, a rather sour, oxidized beer that tastes more like a Vin Jaune from Arbois, France than a beverage fermented from barley. Both beverages owe part of their flavor to the film of oxidative yeasts that forms at the surface of the liquid during maturation in casks. *Vieux lambic* accompanies sauerkraut, fish, and seafood as well as a dry white wine does.

In the late 1800s, the lambic brewer produced about two barrels each of lambic and mars beer from 200 pounds of grain. At 5.5 to 6 percent v/v (4.4 to 4.8 percent w/v), lambic was the product of the first, high-gravity worts, and mars beer, at 3 percent v/v (2.4 percent w/v) was made from the late, low-gravity worts. Faro was prepared by blending varying amounts of lambic and mars beer and sometimes adding candy sugar or cane molasses. The quality of the faro depended essentially on the proportions of lambic and mars used. The best faro, called *half en half* (derived from the English half-and-half), was a blend of equal amounts of lambic and mars. Faro was a sweet, light table beer that had to be brewed and sold before the heat of summer to avoid fermentation accidents and spoilage. In turn, the mars beer used in the faro blends was only brewed until the month of March, from which it derived its name. Today, faro is a blended version of young lambic sweetened with dark candy sugar and caramel and is about 4.5 percent ethanol by volume (3.6 w/v).

6

Gueuze and Fruit Lambics

MICROBIOLOGY OF GUEUZE

To make gueuze, lambics of different ages are blended, roughly filtered, and then bottled. Professor H. Verachtert (1983) and his collaborators followed the evolution and activity of the microbial population in hundreds of gueuze bottles over a one-year period. They concluded that bottle fermentation can be divided into three phases.

The first phase is characterized by the growth of aerobic yeasts such as *Candida, Torulopsis,* and *Pichia,* which likely have their origin in the film formed at the surface of the lambic in casks. The aeration that inevitably takes place during racking, blending, filtering, and bottling operations probably accounts for the growth of these oxidative yeasts. Every effort must be made to keep that aeration to a minimum because these yeasts are responsible for beer gushing. The availability of oxygen can also promote the development of acetic acid bacteria (which are strict aerobes).

The second phase is the longest and most important one. It starts about three weeks into fermentation and is characterized by the fast growth of *Pediococcus* and

Brettanomyces strains. The natural carbonation of gueuze is achieved during that phase.

During the third phase, the density of *Pediococcus* and *Brettanomyces* cells slowly drops until only a few live cells remain in the bottle. Autolysis of the dead cells ensues. It has not yet been established that the presence of pediococci is required for the fermentation to go to completion. Verachtert suggests that these organisms hydrolyze high-molecular-weight dextrins. In the same way as they cause ropiness in lambic casks when present in excessive amounts, pediococci can be responsible for oily bottles. To avoid carrying over a high density of pediococci from the lambic into the gueuze fermentation, it is crucial not to disturb the lees (solids) at the bottom of the casks when the lambics are racked for blending.

GUEUZE

Gueuze is to beer what Champagne is to wine. It is made from a mixture of young and old lambics that is refermented in the bottle. The art of making a good gueuze lies in blending lambics that are one, two, or even three years old. At Cantillon, for example, the brewmaster uses one-third each of one-, two- and three-year-old lambics. Other brewers typically use 70 percent one-year-old lambic and 30 percent two-year-old lambic.

First, the lambics are racked into a mixing tank. Once the mixing tank is full, the blend of lambics goes through a filtration that clarifies it but does not remove all the micro-organisms. Indeed, some microorganisms are needed to referment in the bottle. The blend coming out of the plate-and-frame filter is bottled into Champagne bottles (25 oz) or splits (12 oz) that are made of heavy glass, and the push-up or punt at the bottom gives added strength. The bottles are

Drinking Company. Adriaen Brouwer. Bayerische Staatsgemalde-
samnlungen, Munich, Germany.

corked, metal capped, and then stacked horizontally in the
cellar.

The result of the fermentation in the bottle is a sparkling, fruity, and sometimes dry beer known as gueuze. This
version of gueuze is the authentic, bottle-fermented gueuze,
also called "refermented" gueuze earlier in this text. It takes

three to nine months, including one summer, to make a good gueuze. Warm temperatures are needed to get the fermentation going in the bottle and achieve the right combination of flavors. The alternation of cold and warm periods of 36 to 75 degrees F (2 to 24 degrees C) is a desirable feature during bottle-conditioning, and is indirectly responsible for the special mouthfeel, bouquet, and brilliance of gueuze. This is because the various microorganisms involved in the gueuze fermentation (most of which come from the lambic fermentation) have different optimum temperatures for growth, and because temperature fluctuations precipitate some of the haze components. As the bottles remain undisturbed for several months, yeasts and bacteria settle and die. The following autolysis of the thin film of microbial cells on the wall of the bottle liberates many chemical compounds that also contribute to the unique flavor of gueuze. Gueuze continues to improve for one or two years after leaving the brewery cellars. Some gueuzes may even be aged for five years before they are drunk.

The traditional gueuze-making process is in many ways similar to the *méthode champenoise* used to make Champagne. Champagne begins with a blend of dry white wines called *cuvée* to which fresh yeast starter and sugar are added before it is bottled. A second fermentation in the bottle produces additional alcohol and about six atmospheres of CO_2. One difference in the gueuze-making process, however, is that there is no *remuage* (slowly placing the bottles neck down) or *disgorging* (removing the collected yeast sediment from the bottle). Authentic gueuze is still a live product when it is distributed and it must be handled cautiously. In 1931, more than 3 million bottles of gueuze were lost to hot weather in Brussels.

The other method for producing gueuze is the bulk- or tank-fermentation method, introduced in 1947 by the

DeKoster Brewery (now Belle-Vue). The end of the World War II marked the beginning of the exportation of gueuze to Belgian colonies in Africa. The need for a biologically stable product lead DeKoster to develop *bulk-fermented gueuze*, also called "filtered" gueuze earlier in this text. The selection of the lambics and their preparation for the second fermentation is nearly the same as for bottle-fermenting. The lambics are filtered and blended into fermentation tanks made of inert, non-reactive materials such as stainless steel or glass-coated steel or cement. The tanks, constructed to withstand high pressure, are relatively small by normal industry standards (twenty-five barrels) so that temperature and pressure can be controlled more economically.

The fermentation is ideally conducted at 60 degrees F (15.5 degrees C) and is complete in about two weeks. Carbonation of the beer can be natural or done artificially by passing the proper amount of CO_2 under moderate pressure into beer that is just above freezing temperature. Bulk-fermented gueuze is ordinarily filtered cold and under pressure to remove yeast cells and precipitated materials, then bottled. The filtration is not a sterile one, however, and bulk-processed gueuze is usually pasteurized to stop further fermentation of the remaining extract and to guarantee the microbial stability of the beer.

Further variations of the traditional way of gueuze-making are found within the industry. Some brewers inoculate the lambic blend with a fresh ale starter. Some do not even go through a complete second fermentation before they artificially carbonate the lambic blend, pasteurize it (flash pasteurization), and bottle it. Last, but not least, some brewers have been accused (rightfully so) of blending top-fermented beer with lambic and artificially carbonating the mixture before bottling and labeling their mixture "gueuze."

FRUIT LAMBICS

Kriek, framboise, cassis, muscat, and pêche certainly originated in the days before the hop was used although some of these fruit lambics seem to have developed only recently. Traditionally, fruit lambic is made by macerating whole fruit with young lambic in wooden casks. A second fermentation of the sugars from the lambic and the fruit takes place, and the fermentation cellar becomes quite colorful, with pink, orange, and yellow foam coming out of the casks. The fruit lambic then is matured for several months. It is bottled with some young lambic for natural carbonation in the bottle. Today, there are many variations on this theme, including the use of fruit concentrates, syrups and essences, as well as artificial carbonation in stainless steel tanks, filtration, and pasteurization. Regardless of the way they are produced, fruit derivatives of lambic beers have become very popular with consumers of all ages.

- Fruits -
(Cherry, Raspberry, Peach, Black Currant, Grapes)

The fruits used to make kriek, framboise, pêche, cassis and muscat are cherries, raspberries, peaches, black currants, and grapes, respectively. Some brewers use only whole fruits (and regard their beers as the only authentic fruit lambics), while most of them use a combination of fruits and juices, syrups, concentrates, and essences.

Around the twentieth of July of each year, the lambic brewer gets a call from the local orchards announcing that the crop of Shaarbeek cherries is ready to be added to his young lambics to make kriek beer. Shaarbeek cherries, which

Pouring cherries into the casks ("pipes") to make kriek-lambic. Belle-Vue Brewery.

are now almost impossible to find in the markets of Brussels, are grown in a few orchards of the Payottenland. Small, flat, almost black, very sour, and having a large pit, they are harvested without the stem at a very ripe stage. The harvest is conducted with quavers or trills that shake the tree and detach the cherries from their stems. These cherries offer the right balance of sweetness and acidity and a unique fresh, strong, and natural cherry scent in contrast to the cooked, artificial cherry flavor of most syrups or concentrates. The pulp/pit ratio in these cherries is much lower than in other commercial varieties, so a very high amount of cherries is added to lambic casks (330 pounds or 150 kg per 5.5-barrel cask).

Too few orchards of Schaarbeek cherries are left to supply the entire lambic industry, so Moreno cherries (*griottes*) from Northern France, Belgium, and Germany make up most of the crop used today. These cherries meet the standards of fruitiness, acidity, and pulp/pit ratio required for making kriek lambic.

Sour fruits almost always are preferred for making framboise, pêche, or cassis lambics. As the name indicates, muscat lambic is made with muscat grapes that were traditionally from the local vineyards of the Notre-Dame-Aux-Bois district. Today, they are imported from Italy. Most of the fruit juices used by the lambic trade are pasteurized juices from Germany prepared with a combination of different varieties. Some lambic brewers also have experimented fermenting lambic with bananas or mirabelles (a variety of plum).

Kriek. The sour cherries to be used in kriek traditionally are harvested between July 20 and August 5 in Belgium and Northern France. As soon as they arrive at the brewery, they are poured into clean, empty casks. A 5.5-barrel *pipe* (650 L) receives 350 pounds (150 kg) of cherries and is then filled with 10 or 12 U.S. gallons (40-45 L) of young lambic that is three to eighteen months old. Only 110 pounds (50 to 60 kg) of cherries are used in 2.2-barrel *tonnes*.

The amount of cherries used for lambic varies among breweries. Typically, the small, traditional breweries use more. The brewer must be careful not to use any ropy lambic at this stage because the ropiness may not disappear during the fermentation and maturation of the kriek-lambic. The temperature in old lambic breweries is quite high at this time of the year, and the new fermentation gets under way after about five days and is completed very rapidly (by August 15). The bung-hole is left open for the first two weeks to let the CO_2 from the active fermentation escape. The bung-hole is stuffed with a bundle of small wooden sticks to prevent the cherry pits floating on the top of the beer from plugging it. The sticks are removed and the bungs closed at the end of the fermentation.

The kriek-lambic is then matured in the cask for three to six months. This long maturation is required to extract all the flavor and color from the fruit. Bottling operations usually start around October. Typically, the brewer pumps two *pipes* of first-extract kriek-lambic and two *pipes* of second-extract kriek-lambic into a *foudre*. Second-extract (maceration) kriek-lambic is obtained by a second filling of kriek-lambic casks with the fruit left inside followed by further fermentation and maturation. Some young lambic also is blended in the mixing tank with the kriek-lambic to provide fermentable extract for bottle-conditioning. A suitable ratio usually is two-thirds kriek-lambic and one-third young lambic. The blend is then bottled where it ages from three to five months.

Although krieks refermented in the bottle get better with age, most of them are at their best within a year of labeling. Kriek-lambic should not be kept too long (no more than two years) because it becomes too dry and too high in ethanol and loses some of its cherry character. In addition, its color changes from a dark cherry red to a pastel, tile red.

Framboise, Cassis, Pêche and Muscat lambics. Cantillon's famous framboise is made with 75 percent raspberries, 25 percent cherries, and 0.05 percent vanilla macerated in young lambic. About 440 pounds (200 kg) of the fruit mixture is added to a 5.5-barrel *pipe*, and young lambic is pumped in on top until the cask is full. Other breweries use less fruit, some as little as 110 to 130 pounds (50 to 60 kg) of raspberries per *pipe*. Raspberries get completely decomposed during the fermentation and this can result in filtration problems (mostly due to the pectins in the fruit).

The breweries that produce cassis and pêche use concentrates and essences with a small percentage of fruit. The blend is quickly fermented in two-barrel stainless steel tanks, roughly filtered, bottled, and pasteurized.

For muscat, 330 to 440 pounds (150 to 200 kg) of grapes are added per *pipe*. After the fermentation, three-fourths muscat lambic is mixed with one-fourth young lambic, and then it is filtered and bottle-conditioned.

7

Serving Lambic Beers

STORAGE CONDITIONS

Lambic beers, like other top-fermented beers, are best stored at temperatures from 50 to 59 degrees F (10 to 15 degrees C). Bottle-fermented, corked gueuze and fruit lambics should be stored horizontally, label facing upwards, to keep the cork wet and allow the yeasts and bacteria to settle on the side of the bottle. They should never be opened right after transport. Instead, they should be allowed two to three weeks in the cellar before serving. They will benefit from a month to five years in the cellar depending on the kind of lambic. The temperature of these beers should not be raised or lowered too precipitously or the beers might throw a haze or pick up flavors from the sediment that would be undesirable at this late stage of the aging process.

SERVING CONDITIONS

Lambic has traditional rites and gestures when it comes to drinking it, which ranks it among the aristocracy of beers.

A good way to enjoy a lambic, kriek, or framboise is to get a glassful drafted fresh from the cask in one of Brussels' cafés because of the special care the proprietors provide for these beers. Belgium takes beer serving techniques very seriously. The Office National du Débit de la Bière (ONDB), founded in 1951, promotes the art of drawing off and serving beer by means of courses and training programs. At the end of the training cycle, the successful participants receive a Certified Publican diploma. Their pubs are then regularly visited by ONDB inspectors who check whether the publican continues to serve his beer according to ONDB standards. Lambic is ordered by the pitcher and drafted into a stoneware pitcher at 50 to 55 degrees F (10 to 13 degrees C) so that the customer may pour it at his convenience. A side order of sliced dry sausage or saveloy is customary in Brussels' éstaminets.

For serving at home, when a bottle-conditioned gueuze or fruit lambic is brought up from the cellar, it must be kept horizontal to prevent the sediment from mixing with the beer. A wine basket may come in handy to set the bottle in before pouring.

Different glasses are used for different kinds of lambics. Gueuze is usually served in the traditional, tall beer glass with a straight or inverted-parentheses shape (*verre à gueuze*). A large brandy type glass with a balloon shape closing towards the top is used to drink kriek. Framboise is traditionally served in a flute or Champagne glass. Other lambic beers are served in glasses with a variety of shapes and makes.

Wine corkscrews are perfectly suited for opening bottles of lambic beers. First, the foil covering the top of the bottle is cut off well below the rim. Then, the bottle cap is removed as for a regular beer bottle. The neck of the bottle and the top of the cork should be carefully cleaned to prevent any of the surface material from getting into the beer. Removing the cork can be tricky. Just after corking, the closure is rather

Tavern Interior. Adriaen Brouwer. Museum Boymans-van, Beuningen, Rotterdam, Netherlands.

hard and may stick. Corks that have been bottled several years may become spongy in the center and stick to the sides.

Gueuze might foam out upon opening because of the high CO_2 content and rather warm serving temperature of 54 degrees F (12 degrees C). It is recommended to have an empty glass handy. Gueuze should be poured very slowly, first with the glass tilted, then upright, making sure not to empty the bottle completely because of the sediment. Ideally, the head of foam should be at the meeting point between beer foam and Champagne foam. It usually subsides quickly.

Kriek is traditionally drunk in the summer. It is a very refreshing drink which is best served at 50 to 54 degrees F (10 to 12 degrees C) with a large piece of brown bread covered with cream cheese, onions, chives, and radishes. Some people enjoy kriek as an elegant apéritif over ice. A few years back, it was customary in cafés to give the customer a small dish containing two lumps of sugar and a *stoemper* (a sort of pestle) with his glass of kriek. The customer could balance the sometimes excessive sourness of his kriek by adding a lump of sugar into the glass and dissolving it with the *stoemper*. This practice is still recommended at home when drinking one of the few traditional, dry and sour krieks left on the market. Bulk-fermented or sweetened and pasteurized versions do not require any special treatment and are best drunk at cooler temperatures from 45 to 50 degrees F (7 to 10 degrees C).

Faro should be drunk within a week of purchase, preferably at a cool temperature of 46 degrees F (8 degrees C). *Vieux lambic* is served in a wine glass at 54 degrees F (10 degrees C) like a white wine.

Framboise is served cool at 44 degrees F (7 degrees C). With a little raspberry cream, it makes a great apéritif. Most fruit lambic producers recommend cool serving temperatures for their beers, ranging from 41 degreees F (5 degrees C) for cassis to 54 degrees F (10 degrees C) for pêche.

The standard mechanics of beer tasting apply to lambic beers. The head of foam, color, and clarity of the beer are examined first, then the beer is smelled to evaluate its aroma, and finally the taste, flavor and texture of the beer are evaluated by mouth.

8

Formulations

BREWING LAMBIC

It should now be obvious to the reader that brewing lambic beers is a major enterprise that requires more than patience, time, and expertise. Authentic, true-to-type lambic beers can only be produced in the Payottenland in Belgium because of the presence of a unique microbial flora. This text is not going to change that fact of brewing. One can try, however, to use the information provided here to duplicate the lambic brewing process and brew beers "in the lambic style." But each interpretation of the lambic style brewed outside the Payottenland will have to stand on its own merits.

Out of consideration and respect for Belgian brewers and their lambic products, and out of professional integrity, none of the beers that may be brewed using the formulations that follow should be sold with "lambic," "gueuze," "kriek," or "framboise" printed on the label. It is tempting to use famous appellations to boost consumer interest and product sales. The illegitimate use of the prestigious "Champagne,"

111

"Chablis," and "Burgundy" appellations for mediocre, bulk-processed wines is a good example. Such abuse only creates confusion for the consumer and resentment from the people who produce the real thing (and sometimes law suits, as recently experienced by producers of bulk-fermented sparkling wines). At the same time as we endeavor to duplicate lambic beers as best we can, we embrace the noble cause of small traditional lambic brewers who are fighting for the survival of their product and have embarked on a crusade not unlike the British CAMRA (Campaign for Real Ale).

The guidelines and formulations that follow are the result of an extensive laboratory study that involved brewing trials and fermentation experiments with mixed cultures. In all, about twenty experimental beers were brewed over a two-year period to optimize the formulations. The beers were brewed in the five-gallon pilot plant at the Brewing Laboratory of the University of California at Davis. Compared to other brewing enterprises, brewing lambic beers challenges the homebrewer's and the microbrewer's skills in several ways. It involves the following:

- the use of raw wheat as an adjunct;
- the use of pure, propagated cultures of yeasts and bacteria in a particular sequence for the fermentation;
- the use of oak casks (or oak chips in glass or stainless steel fermenters);
- a great deal of time.

The last point is particularly important. A lambic brew will improve only with time and it will take between six and twenty-six weeks to get the most out of the proposed formulations. In addition, success is by no means guaranteed because of the highly unpredictible behavior of the organisms involved in the lambic fermentation. Having said that, the rewards can be well worth the time and labor.

- A Word of Caution for Microbrewers -

If you cannot afford a separate fermentation and conditioning set-up to brew lambic-style beers, it is best to give up the idea. Introducing a host of microorganisms other than your own *Saccharomyces* brewing strain into the brewery is a very risky business. These "wild" organisms spread very easily to pumps, hoses, and tanks where they do not belong. This point cannot be stressed enough, especially at times when contamination is the main concern of microbrewers.

YEAST AND BACTERIA CULTURES

Since the unique microbial flora of the Payottenland in Belgium is not available anywhere else, it has to be artificially recreated by using pure cultures. Pure cultures can be obtained from the Centraalbureau voor Schimmelcultures (CBS) in Baarn, Holland, or the American Type Culture Collection (ATCC). (Address ATCC orders Atten: Sales Department, 12301 Parklawn Drive, Rockville, MD 20852 USA. Telephone orders should be directed to (800) 638-6597.) The ATCC restricts its distribution of cultures to those trained in microbiology who have access to a properly equipped laboratory. Requests for cultures should show, by a business letterhead, requisition form, or in some other way, that this condition is met. The fee per item is about $45 for non-profit institutions and $60 for commercial firms. Most yeast items also are available from the Yeast Culture Collection of the University of California at Davis (Attn: Mary Miranda, Department of Food Science & Technology, University of California, Davis, CA 95616, USA). Cost is $45 for three items.

When cultures are received in the freeze-dried form, the first step is to recover the culture. A sterile liquid medium (malt extract, wort, water, or MRS broth for bacteria and wort) is aseptically added to the vial containing the culture. After mixing, the contents of the vial are transferred to a test tube containing 6 mL of the proper broth. A loopful of the culture is then streaked onto an agar slant. The culture will be ready for use after a few days unless it is a fastidious (slow-growing) organism.

The medium used should be chosen to suit a particular organism. Wort is perfectly suited for *Saccharomyces, Kloeckera,* and *Candida.* For *Brettanomyces,* some calcium carbonate ($CaCO_3$) must be added to the wort to buffer the acidity produced by the yeast or the culture has a short life span. *Pediococcus* is best cultured in Lactobacilli MRS broth (from Difco in Detroit, Michigan) or wort supplemented with some apple or tomato juice.

To make slants for storage of the cultures, simply add 2 percent agar to liquid broth and autoclave. The medium solidifies upon cooling down. The organisms are propagated by successive transfers in jars of increasing volume.

Cultures of interest to lambic brewers are listed below (the culture type is shown in bold print):

Kloeckera apiculata: **ATCC 32856** (CBS 104).
Pediococcus damnosus: **ATCC 25248, 25249** and **29358**.
Brettanomyces bruxellensis: **ATCC 10560** (CBS 72) and **9775**.
Brettanomyces lambicus: **ATCC 10563** (CBS 75).
Candida lambica: **ATCC 24750** (CBS 1876).

Any number of these should be used in conjunction with a good, pure *Saccharomyces cerevisiae* ale strain. Another option is to harvest the microbial flora of your first successful lambic brew and to reuse it for the next one.

An alternative to the use of pure cultures is to reculture yeasts and bacteria from a bottle of lambic beer. The success of this operation is dependent upon a number of factors. The product must be a bottle-fermented (bottle-conditioned), unpasteurized gueuze or fruit lambic. It must be reasonably young. Most microbial cells die shortly after fermentation in the bottle is completed, and one risks culturing an "incomplete" flora missing one or several of the key microorganisms involved in the lambic fermentation by using an old bottle. This is especially true since the lambic organisms almost all produce high amounts of acids that can cause their premature death (the ecological rationale for such a "suicidal" behavior has yet to be determined).

Many distinguished homebrewers have been successful in the enterprise of culturing yeast from the bottle. A good technique is to funnel sterile wort onto the lees in a freshly emptied bottle, cap it, and thoroughly rouse the mixture (Matucheski; 1989). Be sure to briefly flame the neck of the bottle before and after transferring the wort. The cap is then removed and the bottle fitted with an airlock. From this stage, the culture is propagated by transferring it to fresh, sterile wort in half- and full-gallon jars to build up cell mass before pitching it into the main wort. Problems usually arise at this stage for two reasons: one organism may take over the fermentation and wipe out the rest of the microbial flora, or the mixed culture may die as a result of a low original viability or nutrient deficiency in the wort. The task is not facilitated by the different growth requirements of the various organisms involved. Whereas *Saccharomyces*, *Kloeckera*, *Pichia*, or *Candida* grow fairly quickly after the addition of fresh wort, fastidious organisms like *Brettanomyces* and lactic acid bacteria do not leave their lag phase for a long time and only do so in the presence of a number of growth factors (fatty acids and vitamins). With luck, however, one might get a viable culture of the basic lambic combination *Saccharomyces-Pediococcus-Brettanomyces.*

Additional detailed procedures for propagating and maintaining pure yeast cultures, collecting yeast while traveling, collecting and reusing live brewer's yeast and isolating and culturing yeasts and bacteria from bottle-conditioned beers can be found in the 1989 Special Issue of *zymurgy* on yeast.

BREWING AND FERMENTATION EQUIPMENT AND PROCEDURES

The guidelines that follow apply to "authentic" formulations, that is, formulations with unmalted wheat, pale malt, whole fruits, mixed yeast and bacteria cultures, primary and secondary fermentation in oak casks, and bottle-conditioning. These formulations have a bold-print heading. Other formulations, in which some ingredients are substituted and some steps are modified or skipped, should be brewed using common procedures unless otherwise specified in the "Specifics" section for these formulations.

- Milling -

If brewing at home, crush the wheat and malt with a hand-cranked, Corona-type grain mill. For the malt, use the same coarse grind setting as usual, but for the wheat, make the grind finer. Stay away from flour size, however, because it might result in excessive astringency in the beer.

For microbrewers, mill settings of 0.04 and 0.06 inches are recommended for the wheat and malt, respectively. Mill the wheat first, increase the gap between the rolls, and then mill the malt.

- Brewing water -

If you use water from a municipal supply, obtain a complete analysis (it usually is free) from the water company and adjust the levels of calcium and bicarbonate accordingly. If you have easy access to distilled or deionized water, you should use it. Before brewing with it, add 150 ppm calcium sulfate and 60 ppm sodium chloride.

- Mashing -

The use of unmalted wheat is not common among U.S. microbrewers and homebrewers. The starches inside the wheat are not modified and cannot be mashed in their raw state. They must be gelatinized (solubilized in water) by cooking the grain. Otherwise, the amylases from the malt do not have access to the wheat starches and cannot convert them to sugars. In a cooker, mix the wheat with 10 percent of the malt and bring it to a boil after a fifteen-minute rest at 158 degrees F (70 degrees C). Boil for thirty to sixty minutes with adequate stirring. While the wheat is boiling, start the main mash by mixing the remaining 90 percent of the malt with water. Mash in at 120 degrees F (46 degrees C). Extensive research in our laboratory has shown that there is no significant proteolysis during the so-called "protein rest." It is only justified for β-glucanase action and to achieve a 140 degrees F (60 degrees C) temperature after mixing the boiled wheat in. Mix the contents of the cooker in the mash tun and after a fifteen-minute β-amylase rest at 140 degrees F (60 degrees C), mash at 158 degrees F (70 degrees C) until conversion is complete. Mash off at 170 degrees F (76.5 degrees C) for ten minutes.

An alternative is to introduce wheat flakes directly into the mash tun. The starches in flakes are already gelatinized and are converted by malt amylases in the mash along with the modified malt starches. In that case, a regular infusion mash for one hour at 155 to 158 degrees F (68 to 70 degrees C) is recommended.

- Lautering and Sparging -

At the beginning of lautering, the wort should be very turbid because the mash itself is very turbid, with lots of particulate matter in suspension. Recycle the first half-gallon (10 percent) through the grain bed. The run off will remain turbid but to a lesser extent. Use water at 170 degrees F (76.5 degrees C) at the beginning of sparging and finish with water heated to 190 degrees F (87 degrees C). That will extract unconverted starch granules and husk phenols left in the grains. This practice is undesirable for brewing any other kind of beer but is required for lambic to give the microbial flora a chance to hydrolyze and utilize the in-soluble starch during maturation and aging.

- Wort Boiling -

Boil the wort for about two hours. As long as the gravity of the wort is not too high at the beginning of the boil (ideally 1.030 to 1.032 or 7.5 to 8 degrees Plato), the wort can take a long boil without excessive caramelization. At home, use a large boiler to achieve as low a wort gravity as the formulation permits. An extensive, rolling boil is required to precipitate as much hot break (mostly proteins and some phenols) as possible and to start hydrolyzing some of the complex, high-molecular-weight carbohydrates left in the wort. Only whole aged hops are used to brew lambic because pellets of aged hops are not available on the market. Lambic brewers store hops at room temperature in a dry place for two or three years, but homebrewers can use aged hops that have been stored for a considerable length of time. The hops should be added early into the boil. Hopping rates are given in ounces of hops per five-gallon brew because Homebrewing Bittering Units (HBUs) only apply when fresh hops are used.

- Fruits -

Fruits used in brewing must be clean and perfectly ripe. Bruised, overripe, and cull fruit will not make quality fruit lambics. Use whole fruits, including the pits for cherries. Fruits should be frozen for storage until used.

- Oak Casks -

A new cask has to be "broken in" or "infected" with the proper microbial flora. A good cask, that is, a cask housing the right microbial flora, is one of the keys to many successful lambic fermentations.

Beer casks are available in a variety of sizes, all of which are derived from the British Barrel (1.4 U.S. barrels). The *pin* (5.4 U.S. gallons) is the cask best suited for homebrewers as it is fairly light and accommodates five-gallon brews. The barrel (1.4 U.S. barrels), the hogshead (1.6 U.S. barrels), the puncheon (2.8 U.S. barrels) and the butt (4.2 US barrels) are recommended for microbreweries and brewpubs. Either new or second-hand casks may be used. Small, new or used barrels from wineries also make very good lambic casks.

The first step is to clean the cask. If the cask is lined with paraffin, several washings with boiling water are required to remove most of the paraffin lining. The cask should be soaked with cold water for a few days. Then, about one ounce of soda ash should be added per gallon of cold water.

After two days, the cask should be thoroughly rinsed with hot water followed by a dilute (one teaspoon per gallon) citric acid solution and cold water. Alternatively, the cask may be cleaned with a sodium metabisulfite solution and then rinsed with cold water.

- Fermentation and Maturation in Oak Cask -

Fill the cask with wort right up to the bung-hole. Inoculate with the first culture in the sequence, a top-fermenting ale strain of *Saccharomyces*. The fermentation will be quite vigorous, with a lot of foam coming out of the hole. To avoid contamination, connect a hose to the bung-hole and dip its loose end into a bucket full of water or an empty bottle plugged with cotton wool. After the main fermentation is almost complete (two weeks), inoculate the wort with cultures of *Pediococcus* and *Brettanomyces*. Place the cask on its stillage, gently tap in a softwood peg, and leave the lambic wort to ferment further and mature.

Conditioning or maturing lambics in oak casks is tricky — even for the experienced lambic brewers of Belgium. As explained earlier, in this text, the volume of lambic in the casks drops as ethanol and water are lost by evaporation. The result is the ullage formed on top of the beer. While some transfer of oxygen to the beer and the formation of a film of oxidative yeasts on top of the beer are desirable, too much ullage allows spoilage organisms such as acetic acid bacteria to develop. The problem is less after a month of maturation, when the production of CO_2 has subsided substantially. The ullage should be filled from time to time with lambic from another cask or with fresh wort.

Unless it is going to be used immediately for another lambic fermentation, a freshly emptied cask should be rinsed with hot water several times until the water runs clear. Allow the cask to drip dry and then burn a small piece of sulfur wick through the bung-hole. Close and store the cask in a cool place. Alternatively, to preserve some of the lambic flora housed inside the cask, fill the keg with water after rinsing it clean. The addition of one-half teaspoon of sodium metabisulfite and one-half teaspoon of citric acid per gallon will prevent spoilage.

- Bottle-conditioning -

To bottle-condition the lambic, rack the beer off the cask as you would off a glass carboy, making sure not to disturb the *lees*. The application of a CO_2 blanket to the beer is recommended. Bottle-condition with a freshly mixed culture of *Saccharomyces-Pediococcus-Brettanomyces* and dextrose or corn sugar for priming. Allow four to eight weeks at 65 to 75 degrees F for bottle-conditioning.

The beer might throw a haze if you store it in your refrigerator before serving because it has not been cold-conditioned. This problem can be avoided by racking the beer off the cask into a glass carboy, conditioning the beer at 36 degrees F for a week and then bottle-conditioning.

5-GALLON EXTRACT FORMULATIONS
- Gueuze-lambic -
Ingredients:
> 3 lbs (1.4 kg) pale malt extract
> 2 lbs (0.9 kg) wheat malt extract
> 1/2 lb (227 g) corn sugar
> 1/2 oz (14.2 g) each of Fuggles and Hallertau hops (3 years old)
> Fresh mixed starter culture of Saccharomyces-Brettanomyces-Pediococcus or mixed culture prepared from a bottle of gueuze
> 3/4 cup corn sugar for priming

Lambic

Characteristics:
Original Specific Gravity: 1.044 (11.0 degrees Plato)
Terminal Specific Gravity: 1.009 (2.3 degrees Plato)
Boiling time: 45 minutes
Fermentation: 3 weeks at 64 degrees F (17.5 degrees C)
Conditioning: 1 week
Type of fermenter: glass

Specifics:
Heat water to a boil, dissolve the malt and wheat extracts and the corn sugar. Bring the mixture to a boil and add the hops. Cool the wort to 65 degrees F (180 degrees C), inoculate and ferment in a glass carboy. Rack the beer into another carboy and condition it for a week at a cool temperature. Bottle-condition using the corn sugar for priming.

- Kriek-lambic -

Ingredients:
　　5　*lbs (2.3 kg) light malt extract*
　　2　*lbs (0.9 kg) wheat malt extract*
　3.5　*oz (100 g) corn dextrin powder*
　　1　*oz (28.4 g) of Saaz or Hallertau hops (3 years old)*
　　3　*pints (1.4 L) of pure cherry juice*
　　　Fresh mixed starter culture of Saccharomyces-Brettanomyces-Pediococcus *or mixed culture prepared from a bottle of gueuze*
　3/4　*cup corn sugar for priming*

Characteristics:
Original Specific Gravity: 1.048 (12.0 degrees Plato)
Terminal Specific Gravity: 1.009 (2.3 degrees Plato)
Boiling time: 45 minutes
Fermentation: 3 weeks at 64 degrees F (17.5 degrees C)

Conditioning: 1 week
Type of fermenter: glass

Specifics:
Dissolve the malt extract, wheat extract, and dextrin powder in as much water as your kettle can hold. Bring to a boil and add the hops. Strain hops and bring the volume of the cooled wort to 4.5 gallons. Add the cherry juice, inoculate and ferment for 3 weeks. Rack the beer into another carboy and condition it for a week at a cool temperature. Bottle-condition using the corn sugar for priming.

5-GALLON ALL GRAIN FORMULATIONS

- Light Framboise -

Ingredients:
   7   lbs (3.2 kg) Klages pale malt
   1   lb (450 g) wheat flakes
1 1/2   oz (43 g) Crystal malt (40 degrees Lovibond)
   3/4   oz (21 g) Hallertau or Tettnang hops (3 years old)
   18   oz (510 g) frozen raspberries
   2.5   oz (70 g) sucrose for secondary fermentation
   3/4   cup dextrose or corn sugar for priming
         Sierra Nevada ale yeast culture
         Brettanomyces culture
         Pediococcus culture
         Mixed culture of Saccharomyces-Brettanomyces-
         Pediococcus for bottle-conditioning

Characteristics:
Original Specific Gravity: 1.051 (12.6 degrees Plato)
Terminal Specific Gravity: 1.013 (3.3 degrees Plato)
Boiling time: 60 minutes

Primary fermentation: 1 week at 64 degrees F
  (17.5 degrees C)
Conditioning: 1 week at 36 degrees F (2.5 degrees C)
Secondary fermentation: 2 weeks at 64 degrees F
  (17.5 degrees C)
Conditioning: 1 week at 36 degrees F (2.5 degrees C)
Type of fermenter: glass (oak chips optional)

Specifics:
Mash 15 min. at 130 degrees F (55 degrees C), 10 min. at 140 degrees F (60 degrees C), 45 min. at 158 degrees F (70 degrees C), and 10 min. at 170 degrees F (76.5 degrees C). Inoculate the wort with the *Saccharomyces* culture for the first fermentation. After the first week of conditioning, rack the beer into another carboy containing the raspberries (6 oz raspberries crushed in a blender and 12 oz whole raspberries) and the sucrose. Inoculate the blend with the *Brettanomyces* and *Pediococcus* cultures and ferment for 2 weeks. Rack and condition again before bottling with the fresh mixed culture.

- Pale Kriek -

Ingredients:
  41/4 *lbs (1.9 kg) Klages pale malt*
    4 *lbs (1.8 kg) wheat malt*
  1/2 *oz(14.2 g) each of Hallertau and Tettnang hops (3 years old)*
      Mixed starter culture and sub-culture of Saccharomyces-Brettanomyces-Pediococcus
    5 *lbs (2.3 kg) dark, sour cherries with pits, slightly crushed*
      Lactic acid (85%) to adjust pH to 4.0
  3.5 *oz (100 g) dextrose*
  3/4 *cup dextrose or corn sugar for priming*

Characteristics:
Original Specific Gravity: 1.046 (11.4 degrees Plato) for the
    wort
Terminal Specific Gravity: 1.015 (3.8 degrees Plato)
Boiling time: 60 minutes
Primary fermentation: 2 weeks at 64 degrees F
    (17.5 degrees C)
Secondary fermentation: 4 weeks at 64 degrees F
    (17.5 degrees C)
Conditioning: 1 week at 36 degrees F (2.5 degrees C)
Type of fermenter: glass (with oak chips for secondary
    fermentation)

Specifics:
Infusion mash for 1 hour at 155 degrees F (68 degrees C).
Primary fermentation with mixed starter culture. The cherries, lactic acid and dextrose are added for the secondary fermentation. The beer is racked and conditioned before being bottled with the mixed sub-culture.

- Vanille-Framboise -

Ingredients:
5 *lbs (2.3 kg) Klages pale malt*
3 *lbs (1.4 kg) Wheat malt*
1/2 *lb (227 g) Crystal malt (60 degrees Lovibond)*
3/4 *oz (21.3 g) Hallertau, Saaz or Tettnang hops*
    (3 years old)
1 *oz (30 mL) vanilla extract*
3 *lbs (1.4 kg) whole frozen raspberries*
1 *pint (475 mL) raspberry concentrate*
    (65 degrees Brix)
    Sierra Nevada ale yeast starter
    Mixed starter culture and sub-culture of
    Brettanomyces-Pediococcus
3/4 *cup dextrose or corn sugar for priming*

125

Characteristics:
Original Specific Gravity: 1.050 (12.4 degrees Plato) for the
 wort
Terminal Specific Gravity: 1.015 (3.8 degrees Plato)
Boiling time: 60 minutes
Primary fermentation: 1 week at 64 degrees F
 (17.5 degrees C)
Conditioning: 1 week at 36 degrees F (2.5 degrees C)
Secondary fermentation: 2 weeks at 64 degrees F
 (17.5 degrees C)
Conditioning: 1 week at 36 degrees F (2.5 degrees C)
Type of fermenter: glass (with oak chips for the secondary
 fermentation)

Specifics:
Mash 15 min. at 130 degrees F (50 degrees C), 10 min. at 140
degrees F (60 degrees C), 45 min. at 158 degrees F (70 degrees
C), and 10 min. at 170 degrees F (76.5 degrees C). Inoculate
the wort with the *Saccharomyces* culture for the first fermentation. After the first week of conditioning, rack the beer
into a carboy containing the vanilla, raspberries, raspberry
concentrate and oak chips. Inoculate with the mixed starter
culture of *Brettanomyces* and *Pediococcus*. After two weeks,
rack and condition again before bottling with the fresh
mixed sub-culture and dextrose for priming.

- Gueuze-lambic -

Ingredients:
 6.8 lbs (3.1 kg) Klages pale malt
 3.3 lbs (1.5 kg) wheat
 1/2 lb (227 g) Crystal malt (40 degrees Lovibond)
 1/3 oz (9.5 g) each of Fuggles, Northern Brewer and
 Bullion hops (3 years old)

Saccharomyces *culture (Sierra Nevada ale yeast)*
Brettanomyces *culture*
Pediococcus *culture*
Mixed culture of Saccharomyces-Brettanomyces-
Pediococcus *for bottle-conditioning*
3/4 cup dextrose for priming

Characteristics:
Original Specific Gravity: 1.053 (13.2 degrees Plato)
Terminal Specific Gravity: 1.013 (3.2 degrees Plato)
Boiling time: 2 hours
Primary fermentation (*Saccharomyces*): 1 week at 63 degrees
F (17 degrees C)
Secondary fermentation (*Pediococcus* and *Brettanomyces*): 2
weeks at 69 degrees F (20.5 degrees C) and 4 weeks at 62
degrees F (17 degrees C).
Type of fermenter: oak cask

Specifics:
Mix 1.4 gallons of water at 140 degrees F (60 degrees C) with
the milled wheat and 10 percent of the Klages pale malt. In
a cooker, bring to a boil after a 10-min. rest at 158 degrees F
(70 degrees C). Boil for 30 to 45 minutes. Start the main
mash by mixing 1.7 gallons of water at 130 degrees F (55
degrees C) with the Klages and Crystal malts. Hold for 15
min. at 140 degrees F (60 degrees C). Drop the boiled
adjunct into the main mash, hold at 158 degrees F (70
degrees C) for 30 min. and mash off at 170 degrees F (76.5
degrees C). Slowly run off and sparge. Boil the wort for 2
hours, adding the hops early into the boil. Fill the cask with
cooled wort and inoculate with the *Saccharomyces* culture.
After one week, inoculate with the *Pediococcus* culture and
after three weeks with the *Brettanomyces* culture. Make up
the ullage in the cask every other week with fresh wort. Rack

and bottle-condition with the fresh mixed culture and dextrose for priming.

- Kriek-lambic -

Ingredients:
- 6.8 *lbs (3.1 kg) Klages pale malt*
- 3.3 *lbs (1.5 kg) wheat*
- 1/3 *oz (9.5 g) each of Fuggles, Northern Brewer and Bullion hops (3 years old)*
  Saccharomyces *culture (Sierra Nevada ale yeast)*
  Brettanomyces *culture*
  Pediococcus *culture*
- 10 *lbs (4.5 kg) of dark, sour cherries with pits*
  Mixed culture of Saccharomyces-Brettanomyces-Pediococcus *for bottle-conditioning*
- 3/4 *cup dextrose for priming*

Characteristics:
Original Specific Gravity: 1.048 (12.0 degrees Plato) for the wort
Terminal Specific Gravity: 1.015 (3.8 degrees Plato)
Boiling time: 2 hours
Primary fermentation (*Saccharomyces*): 1 week at 63 degrees F (17 degrees C)
Secondary fermentation (*Pediococcus* and *Brettanomyces*): 2 weeks at 69 degrees F (20.5 degrees C) and 4 weeks at 63 degrees F (17 degrees C).
Type of fermenter: glass for primary fermentation and oak cask for secondary fermentation

Specifics:
Mix 1.4 gallons of water at 140 degrees F (60 degrees C) with the milled wheat and 10 percent of the Klages pale malt. In a cooker, bring to a boil after a 10-min. rest at 158 degrees F

(70 degrees C). Boil for 30 to 45 minutes. Start the main mash by mixing 1.6 gallons of water at 130 degrees F (55 degrees C) with the Klages malt. Hold for 15 min. at 140 degrees F (60 degrees C). Drop the boiled adjunct into the main mash, hold at 158 degrees F (70 degrees C) for 30 min. and mash off at 170 degrees F (76.5 degress C). Slowly run off and sparge. Boil the wort for 2 hours, adding the hops early into the boil. Fill the glass carboy with cooled wort and inoculate with the *Saccharomyces* culture. After one week, pour the cherries into the wooden cask and rack the fermenting wort on top until the cask is almost full. Inoculate with the *Pediococcus* culture and after three weeks with the *Brettanomyces* culture. Save the left over wort into a smaller glass container capped with a fermentation lock and make up the ullage in the cask every other week with it. Rack the kriek off the cherries and bottle-condition with the fresh mixed culture, any beer left over from the primary fermentation and dextrose for priming.

- Framboise -

Ingredients:
   6.8 lbs (3.1 kg) Klages pale malt
   3.3 lbs (1.5 kg) wheat
   1/3 oz (9.5 g) each of Saaz, Fuggles and Alsace hops
      (3 years old)
      Saccharomyces *culture (Sierra Nevada ale yeast)*
      Brettanomyces *culture*
      Pediococcus *culture*
   8.5 lbs (3.9 kg) of fresh or frozen raspberries
    1 oz (30 mL) vanilla extract
      Mixed culture of Saccharomyces-Brettanomyces-Pediococcus *for bottle-conditioning*
   3/4 cup dextrose for priming

129

Lambic

Characteristics:
Original Specific Gravity: 1.048 (12.0 degrees Plato) for the wort
Terminal Specific Gravity: 1.015 (3.8 degrees Plato)
Boiling time: 2 hours
Primary fermentation (_Saccharomyces_): 1 week at 63 degrees F (17 degrees C)
Secondary fermentation (_Pediococcus_ and _Brettanomyces_): 2 weeks at 69 degrees F (20.5 degrees C) and 4 weeks at 62 degrees F (17 degrees C).
Type of fermenter: glass for primary fermentation and oak cask for secondary fermentation

Specifics:
Mix 1.4 gallons of water at 140 degrees F (60 degrees C) with the milled wheat and 10 percent of the Klages pale malt. In a cooker, bring to a boil after a 10-min. rest at 158 degrees F (70 degrees C). Boil for 30 to 45 minutes. Start the main mash by mixing 1.6 gallons of water at 130 degrees F (55 degrees C) with the Klages malt. Hold for 15 min. at 140 degrees F (60 degrees C). Drop the boiled adjunct into the main mash, hold at 158 degrees F (70 degrees C) for 30 min. and mash off at 170 degrees F (76.5 degrees C). Slowly run off and sparge. Boil the wort for 2 hours, adding the hops early into the boil. Fill the glass carboy with cooled wort and inoculate with the _Saccharomyces_ culture. After one week, pour the raspberries and vanilla into the wooden cask and rack the fermenting wort on top until the cask is almost full. Inoculate with the _Pediococcus_ culture and after three weeks with the _Brettanomyces_ culture. Save the left over wort into a smaller glass container capped with a fermentation lock and make up the ullage in the cask every other week with it. Rack the framboise off the raspberries and bottle-condition with the fresh mixed culture,

any beer left over from the primary fermentation and dextrose for priming.

1-BARREL ALL GRAIN FORMULATIONS

- Lambic-style Ale -

Ingredients:
31.5 lbs (14.3 kg) Klages pale malt
15 lbs (6.8 kg) wheat malt
4 lbs (1.8 kg) Dextrin malt (40 degrees Lovibond)
4 oz (113 g) each of Fuggles and Hallertau hops (3 years old)
Ale yeast culture (Saccharomyces cerevisiae)
Pediococcus *culture*
Brettanomyces *culture*

Characteristics:
Original Specific Gravity: 1.049 (12.2 degrees Plato)
Terminal Specific Gravity: 1.010 (2.6 degrees Plato)
Boiling time: 60 minutes
Type of fermenter: stainless steel

Specifics:
Mash in at 142 degrees F (61 degrees C) and hold for 20 minutes. Increase the temperature 2 degrees F/5 min. to 158 degrees F (70 degrees C). Hold for 30 minutes. Mash off at 170 degrees F (76.5 degrees C) for 10 minutes. Lauter with 175-degree-F (79.5-degrees-C) sparging water. Add the hops early into the boil. Inoculate the cool wort with the ale yeast culture and ferment at 64 degrees F (17.5 degrees C) for one week. Rack to another fermenter containing oak chips and inoculate with the *Pediococcus* and *Brettanomyces* cultures. Ferment at 64 degrees F for 4 weeks. Cellar at 36 degrees F (2.5 degrees C) for one week. Filter, carbonate to 2.8 to 3.0 volumes of CO_2 and bottle.

Lambic

- Gueuze-lambic -

Ingredients:
- 32 lbs (14.5 kg) Klages pale malt
- 12 lbs (5.5 kg) wheat
- 4 lbs (1.8 kg) Crystal malt (40 degrees Lovibond)
- 3.5 oz (100 g) each of Fuggles and Northern Brewer hops (3 years old)
  - Ale yeast culture (Saccharomyces cerevisiae)
  - Pediococcus culture
  - Brettanomyces culture
  - Mixed culture of Saccharomyces-Pediococcus-Brettanomyces

Characteristics:
Original Specific Gravity: 1.053 (13.2 degrees Plato)
Terminal Specific Gravity: 1.013 (3.2 degrees Plato)
Boiling time: 2 hours
Primary fermentation (*Saccharomyces*): 1 week at 63 degrees F (17 degrees C)
Secondary fermentation (*Pediococcus* and *Brettanomyces*): 2 weeks at 69 degrees F (20.5 degrees C) and 4 weeks at 62 degrees F (17 degrees C)
Cellaring: 1 week at 36 degrees F (2.5 degrees C)
Type of fermenter: stainless steel for the primary fermentation and cellaring, and oak casks for the secondary fermentation

Specifics:
Mix 140-degree-F (60-degree-C) water with the milled wheat and 10 percent of the Klages pale malt in the cereal cooker. Bring to a boil after a 10-min. rest at 158 degrees F (70 degrees C). Boil for 30 to 45 minutes. Start the main mash by mixing 130-degree-F (55-degree-C) water with the Klages

132

and Crystal malts. Hold for 15 min. at 140 degrees F (60 degrees C). Drop the boiled adjunct into the main mash, hold at 158 degrees F (70 degrees C) for 45 min. and mash off at 170 degrees F (76.5 degrees C). Slowly run off and sparge with 175-degree-F (80-degree-C) water. Boil the wort for 2 hours, adding the hops early into the boil. Pump the cooled wort into the fermenter and inoculate with the *Saccharomyces* culture. After one week, transfer the beer into wooden casks. Inoculate with the *Pediococcus* culture and after three weeks with the *Brettanomyces* culture. Make up the ullage in the casks every week with fresh wort. Transfer the beer to a stainless steel tank for cellaring. Bottle-condition with the mixed culture of *Saccharomyces-Pediococcus-Brettanomyces* and fresh wort.

- Fruit Lambic -

Ingredients:
     31.5 lbs (14.3 kg) Klages pale malt
      15 lbs (6.8 kg) wheat malt
       4 lbs (1.8 kg) Crystal malt (40 degrees Lovibond)
       4 oz (113 g) each of Fuggles and Hallertau hops
           (3 years old)
           *Ale yeast culture (*Saccharomyces cerevisiae*)*
 1.5-2.5 gallons of cherry, raspberry, grape or peach
           concentrate (65 degrees Brix)
           Pediococcus *culture*
           Brettanomyces *culture*

Characteristics:
Original Specific Gravity: 1.049 (12.2 degrees Plato) for the
     wort
Terminal Specific Gravity: 1.020 (5.1 degrees Plato)
Boiling time: 60 minutes
Type of fermenter: stainless steel

Specifics:
Mash in at 142 degrees F (61 degrees C) and hold for 20 minutes. Increase the temperature 2 degrees F/5 min. to 158 degrees F (70 degrees C). Hold for 30 minutes. Mash off at 170 degrees F (76.5 degress C) for 10 minutes. Lauter with 175-degree-F (79.5-degree-C) sparging water. Add the hops early into the boil. Inoculate the cool wort with the ale yeast culture and ferment at 64 degrees F (17.5 degrees C) for one week. Rack to another fermenter containing the fruit concentrate and oak chips and inoculate with the *Pediococcus* and *Brettanomyces* cultures. Ferment at 64 degrees F for 3 weeks. Cellar at 36 degrees F (2.5 degrees C) for one week. Filter, carbonate to 2.8 to 3.0 volumes of CO_2 and bottle.

- Fruit Lambic -

Ingredients:
30 lbs (14.5 kg) Klages pale malt
11 lbs (5.5 kg) wheat
3.5 lbs (1.8 kg) Crystal malt (40 degrees Lovibond)
3.5 oz (100 g) each of Fuggles and Northern Brewer
   hops (3 years old)
50 lbs (22.7 kg) of cherries with pits, or
65 lbs (29.5 kg) of raspberries or Muscat grapes
Ale yeast culture (Saccharomyces cerevisiae)
Pediococcus *culture*
Brettanomyces *culture*
Mixed culture of Saccharomyces-Pediococcus-Brettanomyces

Characteristics:
Original Specific Gravity: 1.048 (11.9 degrees Plato)
Terminal Specific Gravity: 1.016 (4.1 degrees Plato)
Boiling time: 2 hours

Primary fermentation (*Saccharomyces*): 1 week at 63 degrees
  F (17 degrees C)
Secondary fermentation (*Pediococcus* and *Brettanomyces*): 2
  weeks at 69 degrees F (20.5 degrees C) and 4 weeks at 62
  degrees F (17 degrees C)
Cellaring: 1 week at 36 degrees F (2.5 degrees C)
Type of fermenter: stainless steel for the primary fermentation and cellaring, and oak casks for the secondary
  fermentation

Specifics:
Mix 140-degree-F (60-degree-C) water with the milled wheat
and 10 percent of the Klages pale malt in the cereal cooker.
Bring to a boil after a 10-min. rest at 158 degrees F (70
degrees C). Boil for 30 to 45 minutes. Start the main mash by
mixing 130-degree-F (55-degree-C) water with the Klages
and Crystal malts. Hold for 15 min. at 140 degrees F (60
degrees C). Drop the boiled adjunct into the main mash,
hold at 158 degrees F (70 degrees C) for 45 min. and mash
off at 170 degrees F (76.5 degrees C). Slowly run off and
sparge with 175-degree-F (80-degree-C) water. Boil the wort
for 2 hours, adding the hops early into the boil. Pump the
cooled wort into the fermenter and inoculate with the
Saccharomyces culture. After one week, transfer the beer into
the wooden casks with the fruits inside. Inoculate with the
Pediococcus culture and after three weeks with the
Brettanomyces culture. Make up the ullage in the casks every
week with fresh wort. Rack the beer off the fruits into a
stainless steel tank for cellaring. Filter and bottle-condition
with the mixed culture of *Saccharomyces-Pediococcus-*
Brettanomyces and fresh wort.

Appendix

LAMBIC BREWERIES AND THEIR PRODUCTS

List of the breweries that produce lambic beers and related products. Some tasting notes are included. The breweries are listed in alphabetical order, with their complete address, the names of the owner(s) and/or brewmaster, and the brands produced.

Belle-Vue
58-60, rue Delaunoy, 1080 Brussels
Phone#: (02) 522-19-35
Director: C. Vandenstock
Gueuze: very mild; quite fruity; little sourness and a high residual sweetness.
Kriek: strong cherry aroma (artificial cherrylike, as in syrup or bubble-gum); residual sweetness; medium sourness.
Framboise: very drinkable, smooth, light-red framboise with lots of raspberry aroma. A little too sweet and not sour enough.

Brouwerij Bockor
Kwabrugstraat 5, 8540 Kortrijk (Bellegem)
Phone #: (056) 21-65-71
Manager: O. Vander Ghinste
Gueuze Lambic Jacobins: amber color, turbid; strong mousy and butyric characters, not acetic nor sour, in short "incomplete"; slightly sweet.
Kriek Jacobins

Brasserie Frank Boon
Steenweg naar Edingen 238, 1520 Halle (Lembeek)
Phone #: (02) 356-33-99 / 356-12-01
Director: F. Boon
Marriage Parfait: apricot color; turbid; abundant head; woody and green aroma; pungent; very dry, sour and bitter; astringent.

Brouwerij Brabrux
Statiestraat 14, 1870 Wolvertem
Phone #: (02) 269-14-02 / 569-55-92
Gueuze Bécasse: nice volatile acidity (acetic), pungent and spicy aroma; some horsey/sweaty notes typical of *Brettanomyces*; not very sour, no bitterness, some residual sweetness.
Kriek Bécasse: mild and natural cherry character; quite tart and sour; little residual sweetness and no bitterness.

Brasserie Cantillon
56-58, rue Gheude, 1070 Brussels
Phone #: (02) 521-49-28 / 520-28-91
Manager and Brewmaster: J.-P. Van Roy
Lambic
Faro: high volatile acidity combined with caramel and vanilla notes; good balance between sweetness and sourness; light horsey aroma.

Gueuze: amber color turning to brown; turbid; almost flat; very strong wood character; good balance between the fruity (apple cider) notes, the moderate volatile acidity and the mild *Brettanomyces* character; sherry character from oxidation; very dry, sour and astringent; no bitterness. Some bottles have a strong, moldy cork smell (defective); very unique, extreme product.

Vieille Gueuze: nice golden color; high carbonation, foams a lot in the glass but the head eventually goes down; oxidized and acetic aromas; very sour, no bitterness.

Kriek: orange, ruby, dark red color; a very woody nose which overwhelms the cherry and acetic characters; very slight *Brettanomyces* aroma; very sour; astringency from the wood and pits; pungent and sour aftertaste.

Framboise: pink, brown and orange tints and a high carbonation; strong fresh raspberry and oak characters; a touch of volatile acidity but no *Brettanomyces* character; extremely sour; dry and astringent; the raspberry aroma lingers by mouth along with some vanilla and caramel notes.

Muscat: light brownish-orange color; almost still; subtle muscat character; mild sourness; light body; dry, astringent and winey.

Vieux Lambic: perfect example of the style; light amber color; devoid of carbon dioxide; sour and dry.

Brouwerij De Keersmaeker
Brusselstraat 1, 1703 Asse (Kobbegem)
Phone #: (02) 452-47-47
Owners: Paul and André De Keersmaeker

Gueuze: dark golden, sherrylike color; turbid; firm, abundant head that collapses unevenly; typical *Brettanomyces* aroma, slightly sulfury, though; cidery; very sour and dry; high carbonation.

Kriek Mort Subite: bright red color; clear; strong, lasting cherry character (fresh cherry and artificial, chemical-like cherry); slightly sweet and bitter, but not sour; slight plasticlike off-flavor in the aftertaste.

Cassis Mort Subite: brownish orange color; high, fresh black currant aroma; very low volatile acidity and *Brettanomyces* character (made from very young lambic); virtually no sourness but very sweet; slightly bitter; the fruity notes linger in the mouth.

Brouwerij De Neve
Isabellastraat 50, 1750 Dilbeek (Schepdaal)
Phone #: (02) 569-09-02
Director: R. Everaerts

Lambic De Neve: "almondy, aperitif dryness" (Jackson; 1988).

Gueuze De Neve: golden color; stable head; high volatile acidity (acetic acid/ethyl acetate); cidery aroma and *Brettanomyces* character, but on the off-flavor side, i.e., mousy; low sourness.

Kriek De Neve: brownish red color; strong cherry character (cooked cherry/artificial cherry, as in cherry-flavored cough syrups) combined with vanilla and caramel notes; low volatile acidity; pleasant sourness (not too lactic-sour).

Framboise De Neve: very strong framboise aroma (overwhelming), slightly malty, high vanilla aroma; nice sweetness, no bitterness; moderate carbonation.

Brouwerij De Troch
Langestraat 20, 1741 Ternat (Wambeek)
Phone #: (02) 582-10-27
Director: J. Raes
Gueuze-Lambic De Troch: golden color; flat; oak aroma; light-bodied; low bitterness.
Kriek-Lambic De Troch

Brouwerij Eylenbosch
Ninoofsesteenweg 5, 1750 Schepdaal
Director: Dr. E. Hoebeeck
Frater Ambrosius
Faro Extra
Lambic
Gueuze Lambic: nice amber color, clear (filtered); low, stable foam, low carbonation; strong volatile acidity which dissipates quickly; woody and mousy aromas; good balance between the volatile acidity and the *Brettanomyces* character; quite sour, slight sweetness and bitterness (artificial sweetener?); dry but not astringent.
Gueuze Spanik: (filtered) amber color; light aroma; strong and balanced taste.
Gueuze Extra
Gueuze Festival
Kriek Extra

Brasserie Girardin
Lindenbergstraat 10-12, 1744 St. Ulricks Kapelle
Phone #: (02) 452-64-19
Owner: L. Girardin
Lambic Girardin: "big-bodied, fruity and rather bitter" (Jackson; 1988)
Gueuze Girardin: nice golden honey-like color; low volatile acidity combined with a mild to strong *Brettanomyces*

aroma depending on the bottle; well-balanced nose with woody, leather, smoke, spicy and cheesy notes; very sour, with no sweetness; sometimes bitter; very dry (no aftertaste).

Kriek Girardin: purple, dark, ruby red; nice, stable, milky foam; perfect balance between the cherry, oak and pits aromas; almost no volatile acidity but a very pronounced *Brettanomyces* character; barely detectable solvent note; moderate sourness and bitterness; slightly sweet and astringent.

Brouwerij Lindemans

Lenniksebaan 257, 1712 Sint-Pieters-Leeuw (Vlezenbeek)
Phone #: (02) 569-03-90
Owner and Brewmaster: R. Lindemans
Gueuze: (filtered) copper-colored and turbid; low foam stability; very fruity (cherry, peach) and cidery; little volatile

Different labels for the same product (Lindemans Pêcheresse): top: the US label; bottom: the European label.

BOISSON A | FERMENTATION SPONTANÉE
GUEUZE FOUDROYANTE
LAMBIC
IMPORTÉE PAR LES ARTISANS DE LA BIÈRE PARIS | EMBOUTEILLÉE par BRIE LINDEMANS VLEZENBEEK
PRODUIT DE | BELGIQUE | 75cl ℮
09|10|11|12|85|86|87|88| | Conservation minimum 18 mois

acidity, mild *Brettanomyces* character which comes through by mouth; oxidized; medium sourness which dissipates quickly; sweet taste; dry and astringent. Not a strong gueuze but true to type.

Faro Lambic: (filtered) amber, sherrylike color; high carbonation and low, unstable foam; mild lambic aromas (acetic acid and *Brettanomyces* character that comes through as wet wool or warm bread) combined with woody, caramel, vanilla, raisin, prune, yeasty, cooked vegetables and olive aromas; slightly oxidized; quite sour (dissipates quickly, though) and sweet.

Kriek: bright, dark red; very strong (artificial) cherry flavor with some wood; freshly cut grass aroma; no volatile acidity or *Brettanomyces* character; rather sweet; lingering sourness and cherry aroma.

Framboise: dark red, sparkling framboise; the very strong raspberry aroma is on the syrup/concentrate side; some volatile acidity and a slight sourness; too sweet for the style.

Pêcheresse: apricot color with some turbidity; strong peach aroma (between peach yogurt and peach preserves); virtually no *Brettanomyces* character and little volatile acidity; some woody/pit notes; good balance between sweetness and sourness; a very drinkable product overall.
Cassis

Brouwerij van Roy
Nieuwstraat 1, 9380 Lebbeke (Wieze)
Phone #: (053) 21-52-01
Director: R. Thevelin
Kriek & Faro Extra

Brasserie Timmermanns
11, rue de l'Eglise, 1711 Dilbeek (Itterbeek)
Phone #: (02) 569-03-57 / 569-03-58
Director: J. van Cutsem
Lambic
Gueuze: golden, oxidized color; pleasant balance between high fruit, volatile acidity and *Brettanomyces* aromas; horsey by mouth, pungent, not too sour and not bitter; slight tar/wood character by mouth; some residual sweetness.
Kriek

Brasserie Vander Linden
Berendries 1, 1500 Halle
Phone #: (02) 356-50-59
Brewmaster: O. Vander Linden
Gueuze "Vieux Foudre": "full color; dense, soft, rocky head, smooth and dry palate; sour apple tartness" (Jackson; 1988).

Kriek "Vieux Foudre": "lively, with lots of aroma, starting with hints of sweetness and finishing with a dry bitterness" (Jackson; 1988)

Faro Frambozenbier

Duivel: "odd combination of a lambic with a conventional top-fermenting beer" (Jackson; 1988)

Brouwerij Vandervelden
Beersel
Oud Beersel: a very good example of the traditional, authentic gueuze; light brownish amber color; strong *Brettanomyces* aroma and volatile acidity; very dry with hints of wood and pine.

Brouwerij Van Honsebrouck
Oostrozebekestraat 43, 8770 Ingelmunster
Phone #: (051) 30-31-14
Brewmaster: J. Maes
Gueuze Lambic St. Louis
Kriek Lambic St. Louis
Framboise St. Louis

Glossary

adjunct. Any unmalted grain or other fermentable ingredient added to the mash.

aeration. The action of introducing air to the wort at various stages of the brewing process.

alcohol by volume (v/v). The percentage of volume of alcohol per volume of beer. To calculate the approximate volumetric alcohol content, subtract the terminal gravity from the original gravity and divide the result by 75. For example: $1.050 - 1.012 = .038 / 75 = 5\%$ v/v.

alcohol by weight. The percentage weight of alcohol per volume of beer. For example: 3.2% alcohol by weight = 3.2 grams of alcohol per 100 centiliters of beer.

attenuation. The reduction in the wort's specific gravity caused by the transformation of sugars into alcohol and carbon dioxide gas.

bac à houblon. Hop filter.

bac refroidissoir. A shallow cooling tun.

Balling. A saccharometer invented by Carl Joseph Napoleon Balling in 1843. It is calibrated for 63.5 degrees F (17.5 degrees C), and graduated in grams per hundred, giving a direct reading of the percentage of extract by weight per 100 grams solution. For example, 10 degrees B = 10 grams of sugar per 100 grams of wort.

blenders. Companies that contract or buy lambic beers which they ferment, mature, and blend.

Brettanomyces. A strain of yeast in the fermentation of lambic beers that reduces the residual extract and helps give lambic its unique flavor.

carbonation. The process of introducing carbon dioxide gas into a liquid by 1. injecting the finished beer with carbon dioxide;
2. adding young fermenting beer to finished beer for a renewed fermentation (kraeusening); 3. priming (adding sugar) to fermented wort prior to bottling, creating a secondary fermentation in the bottle.

cassis. A fruit derivative of lambic made by macerating black currants in a blend of young lambics.

chill haze. Haziness caused by protein and tannin during the secondary fermentation.

cuve guilloire. Mixing tun.

enteric bacteria. Gram-negative bacteria that are known to produce in wort several sulfur compounds, carbonyls, phenols, and therefore contribute significantly to the flavor of lambic beers.

éstaminets. Belgian cafés or bistros.

faro. A blended young lambic made from moderate-gravity wort and sweetened with candy sugar.

final specific gravity. The specific gravity of a beer when fermentation is complete.

flocculation. The behavior in which yeast cells join into masses and settle out toward the end of fermentation.

foudre. A wooden cask with a capacity of 25 barrels.

fox lambic. Young lambic.

framboise. A fruit derivitive of lambic made by macerating raspberries in a blend of young lambics.

fruit extract. A concentrate or syrup made from various fruits that is sometimes used instead of whole fruit in making fruit derivative lambics.

gueuze. A style in which one-, two-, and three-year-old lambics are blended. One type is "refermented" or bottle-fermented, while another type is "filtered" or bulk-fermented in tanks.

half en half. An old-style lambic made from a blend of equal parts of lambic and mars.

Kloeckera. A yeast strain appearing early on in lambic fermentation.

kriek. A fruit derivitive of lambic made by macerating cherries in a blend of young lambics.

Lactobacillus. A strain of lactic acid bacteria vital in the production of lambic beers.

lambic. A beer style produced from spontaneous fermentation from at least 30 percent unmalted wheat, with a wort gravity of at least 1.020 (5 degrees Plato), traditionally in oak casks.

lambic doux. Sweetened young lambic.

lees. Dik-dik or sediments.

mars. An old-style lambic produced from late, low-gravity worts.

macerate. The process of softening and separating the parts of a substance by steeping it in liquid.

malt. Barley that has been steeped in water, germinated and dried in kilns to convert insoluble starches to soluble substances and sugars.

mashing. Mixing ground malt with water to extract the fermentables, degrade haze-forming proteins and convert grain starches to fermentable sugars and nonfermentable carbohydrates.

méthode Champenoise. A secondary fermentation that takes place in the bottle as used to make Champagne.

muscat. A fruit derivitive of lambic made by macerating grapes in a blend of young lambics.

original gravity. The specific gravity of wort previous to fermentation and compared to the density of water at 39.2 degrees F (4 degrees C), which is given the value 1.000. A measure of the total amount of dissolved solids in wort.

pH. A measure of acidity or alkalinity of a solution, usually on a scale of 0 to 14, where 7 is neutral.

Pediococcus. A strain of lactic acid bacteria vital in the production of lambic beers because it produces lactic acid and causes a pH drop in the wort.

pêche. A fruit derivitive of lambic made by macerating peaches in a blend of young lambics.

pipe. A wooden cask with a capacity of 5.5 barrels.

Plato. A saccharometer that expresses specific gravity as extract weight in a one-hundred gram solution at 68 degrees F (20 degrees C). A revised, more accurate version of Balling, by Dr. Plato.

primary fermentation. The first stage of fermentation, during which most fermentable sugars are converted to ethyl alcohol and carbon dioxide.

secondary fermentation. 1. The second, slower stage of fermentation lasting from a few weeks to years, depending on the type of beer. 2. A fermentation occurring in bottles or casks and initiated by priming or adding yeast.

sparging. Spraying the spent grains in the mash with hot water to retrieve the remaining malt sugar.

specific gravity. A measure of the substance's density as compared to that of water, which is given the value of 1.000 at 39.2 degrees F (4 degrees C). Specific gravity is dimensionless, with non accompanying units because it is expressed as a ratio.

surannés hops. Aged hops.

tonne. A wooden cask with a capacity of 2.2 barrels.

ullage. The empty space between a liquid and the top of its container. Also called airspace or headspace.

vieux lambic. Old lambic, or lambic aged three years in a cask and one year in a bottle.

wort. The mixture that results from mashing the malt and boiling the hops, before it is fermented into beer.

Index

Bibliography

American Type Culture Collection. Catalogue of Strains I. Fifteenth Edition. 1982. Rockville, MD.

Anonymous. 1938. Le Faro. Folklore Brabançon, 103:27-28.

Berger, C. and P. Duboë-Laurence. 1985. Le Livre de l'Amateur de Bière. Robert Laffont, Paris, France. 230 pp.

Brauereien und Mälzereien in Europa 1985. Verlag Hoppenstedt & Co., Darmstadt, Germany.

Centraalbureau Voor Schimmelcultures. List of Cultures. 32nd Edition. 1987. Baarn, Delft, Holland.

Confédération des Brasseries de Belgique. Undated. Belgian beer - A relished tradition - Proven know how. Pamphlet. 46 pp.

Craig, J. T. and T. Heresztyn. 1984. 2-Ethyl-3,4,5,6-tetrahydropyridine - An assessment of its possible contribution to the mousy off-flavor of wines. Am. J. Enol. Vitic. 35:46-48.

De Keersmaeker, J. 1974. Caractérisation de la fraction volatile des lambic et gueuze. Bulletin de l'Association des Anciens Elèves de l'Institut des Industries de Fermentation de Bruxelles, 17:7-11.

Gilliland, R. B. 1961. *Brettanomyces*. I. Occurrence, characteristics, and effects on beer flavour. J. Inst. Brew. 67:257-261.

Gocar, M. 1979. Guide de la Bière. Rossel Edition, Brussels, Belgium. 160 pp.

Gocar, M. Undated. De la Sikaru Summèrienne au lambic Bruxellois. Pamphlet. Musée Bruxellois de la Gueuze. 5 pp.

Heresztyn, T. 1986 a. Metabolism of volatile phenolic compounds from hydroxycinnamic acids by *Brettanomyces* yeast. Arch. Microbiol. 146: 96-98.

Heresztyn, T. 1986 b. Formation of substituted tetrahydropyridines by species of *Brettanomyces* and *Lactobacillus* isolated from mousy wines. Am. J. Enol. Vitic. 37:127-131.

Hough, J. S., Briggs, D. E., Stevens, R. and T. W. Young. 1982. Malting and Brewing Science, Vols. 1 and 2. Chapman and Hall, London, England. 914 pp.

Jackson, M. 1982. Beers of Belgium. Zymurgy, 5(Winter Issue):16-19.

Jackson, M. 1986. Michael Jackson (Editorial). Zymurgy, 9(Winter Issue):15-18.

Jackson, M. 1988. The Simon & Schuster Pocket Guide to Beer. Fireside, New York, NY. 176 pp.

Jocqué, R. Undated. Quand les araignées veillent... dans nos brasseries. Pamphlet. Musée Bruxellois de la Gueuze. 1 pp.

Kreger-van Rij, N. J. W. 1984. The Yeasts - A Taxonomic Study. Third Edition, Elsevier Science Publishers, Amsterdam, Holland. 1082 pp.

La Cambre, G. 1856. Traité Complet de la Fabrication des Bières et de la Distillation. De Lacroix-Camon (ed.), Paris. Vol. I. pp. 349-361.

Malepeyre, F. 1896. Nouveau Manuel Complet du Brasseur ou l'Art de Faire Toutes Sortes de Bières. Encyclopédie-Roret, L. Mulo (ed.), Paris, France. 456 pp.

Malone, P. 1989. Brussels' lambics. All About Beer, 10:32-34.

Matucheski, M. 1989. Scratch brewing the Belgian browns. Zymurgy, 12(Summer Issue):25-29.

Mémoires de Jef Lambic, Les, Editions "La Technique Belge," Bruxelles. Undated. 114 pp.

Miller, D. 1988. The Complete Handbook of Home Brewing. Garden Way Publishing, Pownal, VT. 248 pp.

Noonan, G. 1987. Belgian lambics. Zymurgy, 10(November/December Issue):26:29.

Plevoets, C. and Van Ginderachter, S. 1988. Pamphlet. Musée Bruxellois de la Gueuze. 8 pp.

Riffault, M. M., Vergnaud and Malepeyre. 1853. Nouveau Manuel Complet du Brasseur. Roret, Paris, France. pp. 225-229.

Shimwell, J. L. 1947. *Brettanomyces*. American Brewer, May Issue: 21-22, 56-57.

Spaepen, M. and H. Verachtert. 1982. Esterase activity in the genus *Brettanomyces*. J. Inst. Brew. 88:11-17.

Spaepen, M., Van Oevelen, D. and H. Verachtert. 1978. Fatty acids and esters produced during the spontaneous fermentation of lambic and gueuze. J. Inst. Brew. 84:278-282.

Spaepen, M., Van Oevelen, D. and H. Verachtert. 1979. Higher fatty acid (HFA) and HFA-ester content of spontaneously fermented Belgian beers and evaluation of their analytical determination. Brauwissenschaft, 32:1-6.

Spaepen, M., Moens, D., Heyrman, J. and H. Verachtert. 1981. Enkele nieuwe resultaten van het microbiologisch en biochemisch onderzoek van gueuze overzicht. Cerevisia, 6:23-27.

Vanbelle, M., De Clerck, E. and W. Vervack. 1972. Aspect nutritif de la bière et sa valeur dans la lutte contre l'alcoolisme. Bulletin de l'Association Royale des Anciens Etudiants de Brasserie de l'Université de Louvain, 68:81-94.

Van Oevelen, D. and H. Verachtert. 1979. Slime production by brewery strains of *Pediococcus cerevisiae*. J. Am. Soc. Brew. Chem. 37:34-37.

Van Oevelen, D., de l'Escaille, F. and H. Verachtert. 1976. Synthesis of aroma components during the spontaneous fermentation of lambic and gueuze. J. Inst. Brew. 82:322-326.

Van Oevelen, D., Spaepen, M., Timmermans, P. and H. Verachtert. 1977. Microbiological aspects of spontaneous wort fermentation in the production of lambic and gueuze. J. Inst. Brew. 83:356-360.

Van Oevelen, D., Timmermans, P., Geens, L. and H. Verachtert. 1978. Origin and evolution of dimethyl sulfide and vicinal diketones during the spontaneous fermentation of lambic and gueuze. Cerevisia, 3:59-66.

Van Roy, J. P. Undated. Le lambic et les fruits. Pamphlet. Musée Bruxellois de la Gueuze. 2 pp.

Verachtert, H. 1983. La fermentation spontanée de la gueuze. Cerevisia, 8:41-48.

Vossen, A. 1941. Le lambic. Petit J. du Brasseur. pp. 299-304.

Vossen, A. 1954. Champagne - Gueuze. Proceedings of the "Groupe de Gand des Anciens Elèves de l'Institut Supérieur des Fermentations", Fermentatio. pp. 1-24.

BOOKS for Brewers and Beer Lovers

Order Now ... Your Brew Will Thank You!

These books offered by Brewers Publications are some of the most sought after reference tools for homebrewers and professional brewers alike. Filled with tips, techniques, recipes and history, these books will help you expand your brewing horizons. Let the world's foremost brewers help you as you brew. Whatever your brewing level or interest, Brewers Publications has the information necessary for you to brew the best beer in the world — your beer.

- -

Please send me more free information on the following: (check all that apply)

◊ Merchandise and Book Catalog   ◊ Institute for Brewing Studies
◊ American Homebrewers Association®   ◊ Great American Beer Festival®

Ship to:

Name

Address

City   State/Province

Zip/Postal Code   Country

Daytime Phone (   )

Please use the following in conjunction with an order form when ordering books from Brewers Publications.

Payment Method

◊ Check or Money Order Enclosed (Payable to the Association of Brewers)
◊ Visa   ◊ MasterCard

Card Number   −   −   −   Expiration Date

Name on Card   Signature

Brewers Publications, PO Box 1510, Boulder, CO 80306-1510, U.S.A.; (303) 546-6514; FAX (303) 447-2825

LMBC

BREWERS PUBLICATIONS ORDER FORM
GENERAL BEER AND BREWING INFORMATION

QTY.	TITLE	STOCK #	PRICE	EXT. PRICE
_____	The Art of Cidermaking	468	9.95	_____
_____	Brewing Mead	461	11.95	_____
_____	Dictionary of Beer and Brewing	462	19.95	_____
_____	Evaluating Beer	465	19.95	_____
_____	Great American Beer Cookbook	466	24.95	_____
_____	New Brewing Lager Beer	469	14.95	_____
_____	Victory Beer Recipes	467	11.95	_____
_____	Winners Circle	464	11.95	_____

CLASSIC BEER STYLE SERIES

QTY.	TITLE	STOCK #	PRICE	EXT. PRICE
_____	Pale Ale	401	11.95	_____
_____	Continental Pilsener	402	11.95	_____
_____	Lambic	403	11.95	_____
_____	Oktoberfest, Vienna, Märzen	404	11.95	_____
_____	Porter	405	11.95	_____
_____	Belgian Ale	406	11.95	_____
_____	German Wheat Beer	407	11.95	_____
_____	Scotch Ale	408	11.95	_____
_____	Bock	409	11.95	_____
_____	Stout	410	11.95	_____

PROFESSIONAL BREWING BOOKS

QTY.	TITLE	STOCK #	PRICE	EXT. PRICE
_____	Brewery Planner	500	80.00	_____
_____	North American Brewers Resource Directory	506	100.00	_____
_____	Principles of Brewing Science	463	29.95	_____

THE BREWERY OPERATIONS SERIES, Transcripts
From National Micro- and Pubbrewers Conferences

QTY.	TITLE	STOCK #	PRICE	EXT. PRICE
_____	Volume 6, 1989 Conference	536	25.95	_____
_____	Volume 7, 1990 Conference	537	25.95	_____
_____	Volume 8, 1991 Conference, Brewing Under Adversity	538	25.95	_____
_____	Volume 9, 1992 Conference, Quality Brewing — Share the Experience	539	25.95	_____

BEER AND BREWING SERIES, Transcripts
From National Homebrewers Conferences

QTY.	TITLE	STOCK #	PRICE	EXT. PRICE
_____	Volume 8, 1988 Conference	448	21.95	_____
_____	Volume 10, 1990 Conference	450	21.95	_____
_____	Volume 11, 1991 Conference, Brew Free or Die!	451	21.95	_____
_____	Volume 12, 1992 Conference, Just Brew It!	452	21.95	_____

SUBTOTAL _____

Call or write for a free Beer Enthusiast catalog today.   Colo. Residents Add
• U.S. funds only.   3% Sales Tax _____
• All Brewers Publications books come with a money-back guarantee.   **P&H *** _____
***Postage & Handling:** $4 for the first book ordered, plus $1 for each book thereafter. Canadian and international orders please add $5 for the first book and $2 for each book thereafter. Orders cannot be shipped without appropriate P&H.   **TOTAL** _____

Brewers Publications, PO Box 1510, Boulder, CO 80306-1510, U.S.A.; (303) 546-6514; FAX (303) 447-2825

LMBC

"I read it in *The New Brewer.*"

Jerry Bailey, President,
Old Dominion Brewing Co.,
Ashburn, Va.

Industry leaders like Jerry Bailey know that only *The New Brewer* provides the inside information craft brewers from coast to coast depend on. Each issue is packed with vital statistics for business planning, the latest in brewing techniques, alternative technologies, beer recipes, legislative alerts, marketing and distribution ideas — everything you need to succeed in today's competitive market.

Whether you're an established brewery or just in the planning stages, our in-depth coverage will give you information you can put to work immediately. After all, your business is our business.

The **New Brewer** · YOUR INSIDER'S VIEW TO THE CRAFT-BREWING INDUSTRY